WINDY CITY GHOSTS II
BY DALE KACZMAREK

- A GHOST RESEARCH SOCIETY PRESS P

TABLE OF CONTENTS

CHICAGO'S HAUNTED HOUSES

REFERENCES

INDEX

ABOUT THE AUTHOR

ABOUT THE PUBLISHER

FOREWORD

The windy city is a haunted place. It is ghost ridden by the many who have come to an unfortunate end with its city limits, from its earliest residents to its gangsters and modern, driven businessmen. Chicago has seen it all and more than a few have elected to stay on, as ghosts, for one reason or another, in this special place.

The many ghosts of Chicago come to life in Dale Kaczmarek's newest collection of true haunting tales. His Windy City Ghosts II continues upon the success of the Windy City Ghosts to explore the haunted heritage of this great city as it tells of such strange ghostly places found in all sections of the city. Such places as the Buckhorn Pub where a former owner lingers on after his 1986 death. Dale continues to treat his readers with a blow by blow history of not so much what happens at the haunted spot, but why the ghosts continue to linger there.

Many haunted locations are linked to tragedy, like the 1915 dockside sinking of the steam ship Eastland, where 844 souls lost their lives when the vessel rolled over. The cries of the dying still echo down though time to disturb those walking the waterfront today.

In Windy City Ghosts II Dale Kaczmarek has once again proved himself both a master storyteller and collector of all things haunted. As the sequel to Windy City Ghosts, this newest work expands upon the ghost lore of this great American city. I recommend for anyone who likes a good ghost story and enjoys discovering the little known history of Chicago. But, what ever you do, don't read it at night when the wind blows, the moon shines and bats fly, you may not be able to get to sleep!

Richard Senate
Author of: Hollywood Ghosts and The Ghosts of the Carson Valley.

Introduction

After nearing the finish of my first book Windy City Ghosts, it soon became apparent that no one book was going to cover all the various haunts, stories, legends and supernatural tidbits around Chicagoland. This could take several volumes without doing justice to the immense amount of paranormal events and ghost stories that still remain untold. Through my thirty-one years of paranormal research, I have spoken with and interviewed hundreds and hundreds of people. Some were actual eye witnesses to strange events; others that just passed me on to yet others that had even more to tell about the windy city.

Before and since Windy City Ghosts was released, there have been a number of books relating ghost stories in and around Chicago. While some of these books rehashed some well-known and much related stories, others presented some fresh, new and interesting virgin material. This goes right along with what I've been saying all along.....no one book or volume could hold all the tales of spooks, ghosts, poltergeists and hauntings.

With the Internet becoming ever so popular as the "Information Superhighway", it's becoming so much easier for those to relate their tales of terror and find the right and interested people who will not laugh at them but listen with an understanding of what they've experienced and went through themselves. I receive many emails within the course of a day and hundreds of hits on the official Ghost Research Society website (www.ghostresearch.org) that that alone could probably write a book in itself. Because of the almost instant access and quick responses that emailers get, so much material is swapped on a daily basis. It almost overwhelms the senses and almost puts a burden on ghost researchers, because they are constantly answering questions and replying to their emails.

I knew that almost as soon as I completed my first book, that enough material had already been collected to write a follow-up to Windy City Ghosts and I immediately began to pore over the massive amounts of raw data and stories submitted through the Internet and many leads that others told me. Some, of course, led to dead-ends. This sometimes happens. Others were impossible to trace down because they were nothing more than local legends. However, a vast majority of this data did fan out and lead me to some rather interesting sites.

These sites included restaurants, bowling alleys, cemeteries, churches, private homes and businesses, schools and colleges, historical societies, libraries, theaters, murder sites, department stores and much more. It seemed like every time I turned a corner, I was confronted by another possible haunted site. And, again, I believe that I am only scratching the surface! There are many, many more locations, both public and private that are haunted that haven't yet come to my personal attention. I believe this will happen over time so, needless to say, there will be another sequel to this series of Windy City Ghosts.

My ongoing and tireless research continues to turn up lead after lead which has to be investigated and pored over until the search comes to an end or dead end. I refuse to leave any stone unturned and armed with my computer, the Internet, fellow researchers and members of the Ghost Research Society; we will continue to discover more haunted Chicago.

The most rewarding part of my research is meeting and talking to those many that have actually experienced something themselves. While I remain open to almost anything someone relates to me, I always season their encounters with a dash of skepticism. It's good to be a bit skeptical of what someone tells you, but always keep an open mind. My old adage is "I believe that they believe they experienced something." Who am I to alright dismiss a real and valid phenomenon that someone says they experienced without being there myself? I believe that almost anything is possible in this world today and we just need to be able to accept more of what we hear until we can prove or disprove what they encountered.

The surest way to throw cold water on a possibly great case is to doubt the client's story up front without further study and investigation. While you might not believe, outright, what he or she is telling you, you should at least make an effort to be a good listener and look like you believe it could be possible.

I've heard some pretty outlandish stories in my time and while imagination and sensationalism can be a big part of this, you still need to listen, record and move on with the case. You might be amazed in what you find!

Then there's the story you see on television or cable where there is a repetitive phenomena going on, sometimes in the same room at the same time of day and you wonder, "Why doesn't that person place a camcorder or tape recorder there to document the phenomena?" I often ask that question myself and I guess the answer most often would be that they are simply to frightened or to awed by what's going on to think rationally at the time. Of course, my thoughts would be to immediately try to document and gather evidence for the haunting, while those who are experiencing this bizarre visage, this is the last thought in their mind at the time.

To make my point, I guess what I'm really saying is that no story should be disputed without thorough investigation and research. While natural explanations abound for alleged paranormal encounters, some may indeed be real.

I have followed the same format with this book as I did with Windy City Ghosts. The Chicagoland area is divided into Downtown, North, South and West suburbs. There is also a chapter entitled Haunted House Investigations which documents some of the many true-life haunted houses that I have investigated under the auspices of the Ghost Research Society. Of course the names are changed in each story and only the town or city is listed as an address. This is to protect the privacy of those who may still be living there or others who have since moved in. The last chapter is again devoted to Legends and Short Stories.

These tales may indeed simply be folklore and legends or stories that seem to have no real basis in fact or could not be located. The short stories include those where minimal information was obtained at the time of this printing and no actual eyewitnesses could be located for further clarification.

So, sit back, relax and you browse through Windy City Ghosts 2. You may be surprised at just how close some of these locations are to where you live. Perhaps, it's just outside your back door.

Downtown Haunts

With Chicago being the third largest city in the United States, you would assume that it would also have an inordinate amount of ghost reports and such is the case. I truly believe that Chicago may be the most haunted city in the world! It's not only the stories that I do know about, but the thousands and thousands that I don't. Those that haven't been brought to my attention yet or those new reports of previously known locations could run well into the thousands easily.

People who have had encounters with the supernatural are becoming much more at ease in discussing their experiences now than in previous decades. The way that ghost researchers and even the media treat such reports surely has to be the determining factor in the drastic increase of sightings. Witnesses feel that need not be ashamed or even fearful of laughter or ridicule when they relate what they have seen or heard. While ghost researchers have a lot to do with this increase, I truly believe that programs such as Haunted History, Sightings, Unsolved Mysteries and others have drawn eye witnesses "out of the closet" and into the light of respect and dignity. Something that wasn't so evident in years gone by.

Ghostbusters may have started it, but the trend is definitely for finding actual evidence in the form of pictures, video or audio tape and the use of high-tech equipment. Ghostbusters broke new ground when it came out and it doesn't show any sign of letting up. In fact, documentaries are getting better and better through experience in film making.

Many documentaries have been made here in the Chicagoland area in recent years as producers realize that there is a treasure trove of stories here in a never-ending supply. Some of the following tales may be familiar but I will guess that the majority will be new to you, even those who live in Chicago and its environs. Let's get right to work and explore the haunted Windy City!

Bucktown Pub
1658 W. Cortland Street
773-384-1408

The area where this drinking establishment is now located is called Bucktown and in the early history of Chicago, before Chicago was Chicago, area residents raised and kept goats on this land. Dating back to the 1830s, the area is now home to a very unique pub where you almost step back into time. Back to the 1960s and 70s that is. The interior is literally adorned with memorabilia from that era including posters, autographed pictures of famous people and even comic book art, all meticulously collected and displayed by Mike Johnson, a Chicago area archivist and collector.

Current owner, Krystine Palmer, prides herself in being able to have twenty-one different types of beers on tap and to live with a ghost as well.

The ghost is thought to be a former owner named Wally who lived there with his wife, Annie until one day in 1986; he put a gun to his head and blew his brains out in his upstairs bedroom, directly over the downstairs bar. After that bit of trauma, the bar remained empty for a number of years until Krystine Palmer bought the place from his widow in 1991. They completely redid the place into what it looks like today.

Soon poltergeist-type phenomena began to plague the bar including things rearranging themselves without human assistance. Bottle of booze, napkins and napkin holders as well as coasters were always found in different positions in the morning as if someone didn't like the way they were arranged the previous evening. Sometimes visions would be seen by people out of the corner of their eyes. Visions that disappeared when you would turn your head to investigate who or what was there.

Other times the jukebox would malfunction. Sometimes turning itself completely off or refusing to play certain record selections. Apparently the ghost has his own taste in music too. One employee had a beer sign fall on him for no apparent reason. He quit soon afterwards, not wanting to try his luck on something heavier.

According to those who remember Wally, he wasn't all that nice of a person, often rowdy and mean. He was said to be verbally abusive to both employees and sometimes customers. Frequently he would throw chairs and other objects around. Perhaps that's the reason the levitating objects continue to this day? Maybe his energies are still around causing trouble and worry to those who must work at the pub.

If you plan to visit the pub, don't get too concerned if you see something fly across the room with no one to propel it. It's just Wally having another bad day.

Eastland Disaster
Wacker Drive between Clark and LaSalle Street Bridges

Chicago has been known for disasters, loss of life and violence in the past. Chicago's worst disaster to date was the capsizing of the *SS Eastland* on July 24, 1915. Estimates range as high as 844 people who drowned just a few feet from the loading ramp or below decks when the heavily-overloaded pleasure boat spilled to one side.

The *Eastland* was in 1903 for the Michigan Steamship Company and was officially launched on May 6th. The *Eastland* was designed as a twin-screw ship with high-rising steel sides and a fender strake, as distinct from a steamboat with overhanging guards and a wooden superstructure. The ship was designed to carry 2,000 passengers with sleeping accommodations for 500, however, on July 2, 1915; this was upgraded to 2,500 with the addition of three boats and six rafts. The gangways were built so low that, from the outset, the ship had a small range of lateral stability. When the aft gangways were 18 inches above the waterline, a list of only some 7.5 to 10 degrees was enough to bring water onto the main deck.

She was side-launched at 2:30 p.m. into the Black River at Port Huron and christened by Frances Elizabeth Stufflebeam. The *Eastland* eventually began to make runs between Chicago and Michigan City, Indiana and South Haven, Benton Harbor and St. Joseph in Michigan.

Since 1911 the Hawthorne Club in south suburban Cicero, Illinois had organized an annual picnic for employees of Western Electric in Michigan City, Indiana. The club arranged for the excursion each year with Walter K. Greenebaum, president and general manager of the Indiana Transportation Company.

Saturday, July 24, 1915 was the day of the annual company picnic. Seven thousand tickets were distributed to company workers and their families living in the Chicago area. The tickets were seventy-five cents each and children were to be admitted at no cost.

That morning, the *Eastland* was moored from its starboard side to docks on the south side of the Chicago River near the Clark Street Bridge. The *Theodore Roosevelt*, the *Petoskey*, the *Maywood*, the *Racine*, and the *Rochester* were other ships chartered for the picnic and moored near the *Eastland*. Specific ship assignments had not been made for the employees. So, because the *Eastland* and the *Theodore Roosevelt* were the newest and most elegant, most Western Electric employees wanted to board these ships. And since these two ships were scheduled as the first to depart, there was little doubt that both would be filled to their capacities.

Built of steel and four decks high, the ship's nickname was "Speed Queen of the Lakes." Its 22-mile-an-hour slice through the water was due to its unusually narrow width of 36 feet. Sure, there had been rumors of its instability, but there had been the dare offered by one of the ship's owners; a $5,000 reward for the man who could prove that the Eastland was unsafe. No one took the bait.

At 6:30 a.m., preparations began for loading. The river was fairly calm. There was no wind and the skies were partly cloudy. The *Eastland* was scheduled to depart at 7:30 a.m. At this time, 5,000 people had already arrived and were waiting to board, so when the gangplanks were lowered, people rushed in so that they would not be denied a chance to ride the Eastland. The majority of those preparing to board the ships were actual employees of Western Electric. Because the company picnic was an important social event, a great many of the employees in attendance were young, single adults in their late teens or early 20s.

At 6:40 a.m., passengers began boarding the ship. At 6:41 a.m., the ship began to list to starboard (towards the dock), but this was not unusual as it was due to a concentration of boarding passengers who had not yet dispersed throughout the ship and were lingering on the starboard side. But, as the list hindered the continuation of loading slightly, the *Eastland's* Chief Engineer, Joseph Erickson, ordered the port ballast tanks to be filled to help steady the ship. By 6:51 a.m., the ship evened out.

At 6:53 a.m., the ship began to list again, this time to port. When the list reached 10 degrees, Erickson ordered the starboard ballast tanks to be partially filled. The list was straightened temporarily, but, as passengers were loading at an approximate rate of 50 per minute, the passenger count had reached capacity by 7:10 a.m. At this time, the ship began to again list to port. The port ballast tanks were emptied, but the port list increased to approximately 15 degrees by 7:16 a.m. Within the next few minutes, the ship straightened again, but the port list resumed at 7:20 a.m., at which time water began coming into the ship through openings on the lower port side. Even so, no great panic occurred among the passengers. In fact, some began to make fun of the manner in which the ship was swaying and leaning.

While this was occurring, the gangplank was closed and most passengers on the ship migrated to the port side where they had a view of the happenings on the river rather than a view of the dock. By 7:23 a.m., the list had become too severe that the crew directed passengers, many of whom were on the ship's upper decks, to move to the starboard side. However, by 7:27 a.m., the list had reached an angle of 25 to 30 degrees. More water began to flow into the ship from openings in the port side, and chairs, picnic baskets, bottles and all sorts of items began to slide across the decks. Still there was no general panic. The band on the *Theodore Roosevelt*, playing "I'm on My Way to Dear Old Dublin Bay," could be heard on the open decks.

At 7:28 a.m., the list had reached 45 degrees. At this point, many of the crew began to realize the seriousness of the situation. Many more passengers were now on the port side of the ship, as they had gone there to view a passing Chicago fire boat that had sounded its whistle while passing. As the furnishings and appliances on the boat fell over with loud crashes and slid across the decks, the passengers began to panic. Many passengers began to crawl out of gang ways or other openings on the starboard side as the Eastland gently continued to list to port until it finally settled on its port side at 7:30 a.m.

Some passengers who had pulled themselves to safety were fortunate to find themselves standing on the starboard hull of the Eastland. Others who were not so lucky were trying to stay afloat in the currents of the river. Others were trapped within or under the *Eastland*. One eyewitness described the scene:

"I shall never be able to forget what I saw. People were struggling in the water, clustered so thickly that they literally covered the surface of the river. A few were swimming; the rest were floundering about, clinging to a life raft that had floated free, others clutching at anything that they could reach - at bits of wood, at each other, grabbing each other, pulling each other down, and screaming! The screaming was the most horrible of all."

Other boats in the area and people nearby began helping with rescue operations immediately. Some onlookers dove into the river or jumped onto the boat to help those who were struggling while others threw wooden planks and crates into the water to help people stay afloat. The crews of other ships were pulling people out of the water, dead and alive. By 8 a.m., all survivors had supposedly been pulled out of the river. Ashes from the fireboxes of nearby tugboats were spread over the starboard hull of the *Eastland* so rescue workers would not slip on the wet and slick surface as they cut holes in the side of the hull to pull out survivors as well as dead. The screams coming from those inside the ship were disturbing for onlookers. By the time the holes were cut in the hull, many who had been alive at the time the ship rolled had since drowned. A great effort was expended to remove the dead from inside the ship as divers had to go underwater within the hull to retrieve bodies.

A major problem occurring immediately after the disaster was the vast amount of bodies that needed to be laid out in order to be identified. As the Western Electric employees were not assigned to ships, no passenger lists existed and none were written as the ship was boarded. By Saturday afternoon, the Second Regiment Armory on Washington Boulevard had been established as the central morgue. The bodies were set together in rows of 85 and around midnight on the 24th, those who believed their relatives might have perished were admitted to begin identifying. Identification took a few days since 22 entire families were wiped out in the disaster and no one was left in the immediate area to assist in identification.

The total death toll was 844 people. Eight hundred and forty-one were passengers, two were from the crew, and one was a crew member of the Petoskey who died in the rescue effort. Although the *Titanic*, which sank three years before in 1912, had a higher total death toll of 1,523, the *Titanic* actually had a lower death toll of passengers than the *Eastland* as crew deaths from the Titanic totaled 694. And, the ironic part is that all these people died in just 20 feet of water in downtown Chicago, just a few feet away from the safety of the dock and dry land.

Salvaging the ship was not an easy task. While raising the ship, difficulties were encountered in getting it to float as so much water needed to be pumped out of the hull. The ship was finally refloated on August 14th.

The *Eastland* was acquired by the Illinois Naval Reserve four years later, after several modifications which enabled the ship to serve safely as a training vessel. The ship, re-named the *U.S.S. Wilmette*, served for several years until it was decommissioned in 1945. The ship was then sold for scrap, and by early 1947, the ship was completely disassembled for parts and metal.

A bronze plaque was erected on the site, Sunday, June 4, 1989 and there were thought to be only four survivors alive from the disaster. However, only Libby Hruby, 84 at the time, was in sufficiently good health to attend the ceremony.

For a number of years now the area where so many lost their lives has been the scene of strange paranormal activity, namely sights and sounds. Pedestrians strolling past the site, particularly in the evening, often hear a loud commotion in the water as though a number of people are floundering around. Screams and splashes are the most often encountered type of sound heard by people near the area. Of course, when they look from the overlook, they see nothing amiss and the water perfectly calm.

Some have seen a large wash of water suddenly overflow the river walk area of lower Wacker Drive where there are a number of riverside cafes. Such would have been reminiscent of the water that was thrown on the lower docks when the *Eastland* rolled over. Those who have availed themselves an afternoon stroll along the river or have stopped for lunch at one of the many cafes have been shocked to see something actually in the water. On closer inspection, they have complained of seeing strange reflections of faces, not their own, staring back at them from the depths of the Chicago River. Obviously victims of the unfortunate accident.

It may take quite sometime for the energies to dissipate sufficiently for the paranormal activity to cease altogether. Until then, the ghosts of the *Eastland* will be encountered.

Erie Street House (former)
Erie Street and Seneca
Chicago, IL. 60611

At one time the corner of Erie Street and Seneca was a parking lot where Chicago Motor Coach buses checked in and out every hour of the day and night. The neighborhood was one of artist's studios, shops and rooming houses which had followed the old families who once lived on Erie Street at the turn of the century.

Many Chicagoans now living recall the large double stone front houses which stood vacant in this once fashionable neighborhood in the late 1890s surrounded by tenanted and spacious houses. The basement windows were boarded up and although enterprising agents attempted to rent the place, the efforts were futile. No tenant could be found, for neighbors spread the word that the place was haunted and that ghosts roamed through the spacious halls and vast rooms.

Strange noises were heard at night, and the sound of a heavy carriage stopping in the dead of night in front of the house caused more than one adjacent home owner to peer out of the window at the midnight callers.

In 1898, the police investigated with no results. Though neighbors all claimed to have heard the carriage, no one had ever seen it. Neither carriage nor wheel tracks were ever visible the next morning.

When anyone investigated the house, it always stopped. If not disturbed, however, the queer grating sound of a heavy box being removed from a vehicle was heard, and then mysterious footsteps approached the house and disappeared within.

Little children of another generation who peered over the high fence in the rear of the place discovered ghastly bones which their parents declared were human! This was no idle surmise for the last occupant of the double house at 272 and 274 Erie Street had been the old National Medical College (later at Wells and Schiller) and it was a fact that the medical students had carelessly thrown the bones in the yard.

The ghostly tales that neighbors told about the "haunted house" undoubtedly originated from the activities of those medicals students.

Nearly every night during the college year, a mysterious wagon would draw up to the place and deposit a cadaver. Quite often the bodies were wrapped loosely in a sheet and their ghastly faces could be seen. Then all night the neighbors were treated to boisterous laughter, mingled with the sawing of bones and the wild shouts of hilarious students. The bones of the stiffs were thrown into the rear yard and the grinning skulls greeted those whose windows looked down upon the place.

It was the firm belief of many who lived on the near North Side that the troubled spirits of these subjects whose bodies were used to benefit science returned to protest the way in which their bones were treated.

Excalibur
632 N. Dearborn St.
Chicago, IL. 60610
312-266-1944

Architecture has always meant a great deal to Chicago and many fine examples of old buildings can still be found in select areas if one knows where to look. One of the city's few remaining and best examples of Romanesque Revival architecture is the monumental, picturesque-styled structure which was designed by one of the era's most successful architects. It is generally considered one of his finest works.

Romanesque Revival was derived from 11th and 12th Century architecture of France and Spain and was often associated with heavy, rough-cut stone walls, round arches and squat columns with deeply recessed windows and pressed metal bars and turrets.

The famous architect, Henry Ives Cobb, (1859-1931), designed the second Chicago Historical Society building in 1892. The Chicago Historical Society occupied the building from the 1890s until 1931; it was that organization's need for a fireproof structure that accounts for the building's granite-clad construction. The buildings later uses included the prestigious Institute of Design and recording studios for influential blues and rock n' roll performers in the 1950s and '60s.

Cobb arrived in Chicago in 1881 and had received several significant commissions in the Chicago area, including the Newberry Library, the Chicago Opera House and Lake Forest College. Born in Brookline, Massachusetts, in 1859, he had finished a preparatory course in architecture at Massachusetts Institute of Technology in 1880, and then transferred to Lawrence Scientific School at Harvard where he obtained his degree. Following in the footsteps of other noted architects, Cobb went abroad to study at the Ecoles des Beaux Arts in Paris, France.

After the Chicago Historical Society moved its headquarters to the Lincoln Park area, the building was used for various purposes including the Loyal Order of Moose, the WPA, the Illinois Institute of Technology and Gallery Magazine. A nightclub Limelight operated there in 1985 until Fred Hoffmann purchased the building in 1989. Since then it's been known as Excalibur and Aura.

Just after opening as the Limelight, it was alleged that the building was considered to be haunted. Poltergeist activity, in particular, was encountered on the third floor landing of the Dome Room by the former Special Events Director. Things would fall over by themselves and glasses would often fall and break without any living persons nearby. Pool balls would move around certain pool tables as though "someone" was having at a game and employees would often hear their names being called in the empty building by someone they didn't recognize.

The sounds of large crates or boxes were heard being dragged around the downstairs storage room but when opened, nothing was amiss. Cold spots were reported in the past in the women's restroom which was later plagued by crying sounds and faucets turning on by themselves.

The building is comprised of approximately 45,000 square feet, 17,000 of which were added in renovations. The name "Excalibur" was derived from King Arthur's magical sword while "Aura" was the Chicago Historical Society's lecture hall/auditorium. Within Aura, sometimes referred to as the "Dome Room" is a mural of the mythical god Zeus which was created by Paseka which stares down upon patrons within the room.

There are many rumors and legends associated with this location including that some of bodies from the Eastland tragedy were brought here and temporarily stored in the Dome Room. This author was unable to verify this alleged fact to the present, but if it were true would account for a variety of haunting phenomena still occurring within the ancient walls.

The paranormal television show *Sightings*, hosted by Tim White, did a segment here in 1997 with psychic Jorianne De'Frey and, ghost hunter, Peter Moscow. They apparently were also told that the *Eastland* victims were brought here in small numbers. The psychic was quoted as hearing a child's voice saying, "Stop and watch me." (However no records indicate that the building was ever used for such a purpose.)

Waitress, Julia Rosenwinkel at the time of the segment, heard a really small voice crying while washing her hands in an upstairs bathroom in the Dome Room. Bartender, John Karrer, saw a white tuxedo figure reddish hair glowing behind a bar which once existed on the east end of the room.

Creative Director, at the time, Tom Neubauer smelled the most horrible stench of death, thought to be rotting flesh that almost made him pass out it was so intense. It was rumored that a man jumped from the former building to save his life during the Great Chicago Fire of 1871 and that his ghost may be one of those encountered there from time to time.

Employees complain of candles relighting themselves in just a few seconds after having been blown out in preparation of closing the room. An apparition of a small child has been seen on several occasions leaning over the second floor railing of the Dome Room. When eye witnesses look back a few moments later, she is gone. Surely what was seen was not legal age of entry to this establishment.

Billy McFall, Excalibur's corporate supervisor, spoke of a number of strange and unusual events during a 1996 Chicago Sun-Times article. Beer glasses were often found scattered about by the opening crew even though the motion detectors had not been set off by the motion. A light blue colored figure of sorts was observed on two occasions floating up the stairs by McFall.

One other alleged possibility is the persistent rumor that early Chicagoan John Lalime who lived very peacefully on a section of land on the banks of the Chicago River may haunt the club. Lalime's property was seized in 1803 by John Kinzie and Lalime was eventually killed by Kinzie and buried in Kinzie's own backyard; the same property that he grabbed from Lalime. Lalime's bones were much later brought to the first Chicago Historical Society. Could Lalime's ghost be yet another attributed to Excalibur? How about the reports of a lawyer allegedly committing suicide on the site?

There may be quite a number of ghosts roaming her from many generations of Chicago's past. Who knows how many more may become attracted to the place in the future?

Even though this is quite a bit of psychic activity being reported to present day at Excalibur, it has nothing at all to do with the Eastland disaster. Some may say that this building was used as a temporary morgue however the book detailing the history of the Chicago Historical Society shows no such record of such an event and since this abode was a former Chicago Historical Society structure, surely such a terrible event would have been listed in the past history.

Gold Star Bar
1755 W. Division St.
Chicago, IL. 60622
773-227-8700

The Gold Star is a sixty-year-old plus bar located in Wicker Park, Chicago. In the old days, people traveled from all over the United States, to visit "Polish Broadway", the strip of bars between Ashland and Western avenues which include one mile of bars and cocktail lounges, in which to sing and dance the night away. Couples had a drink a one bar, and then would promenade to the next. Patrons during this era included Al Capone's brother, and FBI men at the other end of the long mahogany bar.

In the 1960s, this area had a bad reputation for hookers and dancers soliciting customers to the backrooms and dirty upstairs for a little "extra". There have been murders reported here over the years, including one that took place in the 1950s. A former bartender killed a thief attempting to rob the place near the front door of the tavern. Employees have felt uncomfortable in this area of the establishment and occasional glimpses of "something" in the corner's of their eyes is also quite common.

The lounge was bought in 1990 by three men who tried to change its character to something a bit more respectable. They have certainly accomplished this. The hookers, dope-addicts and rift-raft are gone and the upstairs apartments are now occupied by normal people. However this hasn't apparently stopped the paranormal activity one bit.

Lights often go off by themselves, especially in the back rooms. Not simply a fuse or a burnt bulb, but apparently the switch itself being physically switched off by unseen hands. Electric contraptions are also the play toys of the ghost including stereos and televisions that appear to have a mind of their own.

Another veteran employee of the bar has actually seen an apparition as clear as a living person standing next to her one evening. She described the ghost as female and wearing a bright green dress. She disappeared when given a second glance.

A patron alleges that he saw a spirit of a man dressed like a farmer with suspenders and a banded straw hat disappear into the men's room. There's only one door in and out, and he never came back out!

No one has any idea who these spirits are but they have been seen for quite awhile and show no signs of going away anytime soon.

Granny
Chicago, Illinois

Some years ago on one of the west side boulevards, there stood back from the street a large square house of buff brick, the home of a widow, her three children and their grandmother.

"Granny" was a Scotchwoman. In the past there had been warlocks in the family; there was second sight in the blood; and it was a legend that in the reign of James VI an ancestor had paid at the stake the price of sorcery.

Granny's favorite grandchild was the youngest son Charley - a wild unruly boy of 18. One evening at the dinner table, Granny did not touch her food. With her stiffened hands resting against the table edge, she sat staring straight before her.

"The lad won't be home this night," she said, "not till morning. He has met with evil companions and gone into evil ways. I see it all as my father before me saw many a thing far off. They came and Charley listened to them and they're drinking around a table, and I can see the cards in their hands through the smoky air."

Morning did bear Granny out. It was dawn before Charley returned flushed and incoherent.

There followed many nights when the grandmother walked the halls, the mother and sisters waiting in the bedrooms upstairs and listening to the slow tread, hard on the waxed floor, muffled on the rugs.

That winter Granny died and Charley, penitent in his grief reformed, until spring. Then he went back to his old ways and his old friends.

The neighbors first began to wonder when the servants left the buff-colored house, two settled women who had grown middle-aged in the service of the family. Two new servants stayed but a short time. One, an elderly Irish woman, was asked why she left so desirable a job.

"I don't like a place where you find the cat dead of a morning," she explained, "dead standin' back in a corner of the hall, the hair stickin' out from her body, and her eyes starin' back in fright."

The old police dog leaped over the cast iron fence one night and was never seen again. The little terrier refused to stay indoors at night and stood trembling until morning on the back porch. These were the nights when Charley was out with his wild companions.

For a reason unexplained to the neighbors, the tiling was removed from the floor of the vestibule and a long plush carpet laid the length of the upper hall but still no servant stayed longer than a week in the buff-colored house.

One night during a party at the house, Granny's fearful footfalls were heard again on the hard polished floor, soft as if on rugs; slow and labored on the stairs; then muffled on rug again. Down the steps they sounded, hard on the floor that was actually buried under plush pile and sharp on tiles where no tiles were. The footfalls ceased.

The party broke up hurriedly, only a few of the older friends of the family remaining. They huddled together in the parlor. Toward midnight, a shriek sounded through the rooms. Granny's voice! Three times the awful cry of pain and fear and then one long deep groan.

It wasn't long before they heard the resounding clatter of horses hoofs fast driven. The mother rose and opened the door only to see the white uniforms of the ambulance interne and attendants.

The younger sister shrieked and Charley was borne down the hallways with a covered face. No one asked where or how he met his death. They had felt it in Granny's screams. She had seen it all in the eyes that had peered too far away, the smoky air, the strewn cards, the upturned table and the tavern brawl.

Charley was buried beside his father and grandmother in Graceland Cemetery and the mother and sisters continued to live in the buff-colored house on the West Side Boulevard. Granny walks its halls no more.

Hangge-Uppe Tavern
14 W. Elm St.
Chicago, IL. 60611
312-337-0561

This tavern has been in the Rush Street area for quite sometime henceforth the name and is host to young people who particularly like the music from the 1960s and 1970s even though all types of music is played including the modern stuff.

Before being converted into a bar, allegedly it was used as a mob front. They apparently used to conduct their illegal business in the basement, now the new part of the bar.

A former employee named Carl tells of his encounter, "One afternoon I started work at 4:00 p.m. I went downstairs to use the restroom when I heard a noise from the female restroom around the corner. I started to shout, 'Who's here?' no answer. About five minutes later one of the cleaning guys came back in the building. I asked if he was next door and he replied no. We went to check it out and the shutter stall doors were swinging! He said it was the wind. Yeah, right. I asked if he believed this place was haunted. He didn't answer. About two seconds later, a glass from the second top shelf fell off, hit the cash register, and landed straight up on the sill of the register. There were no cracks or chips in the glass at all. He started to stutter.

"One night after closing, I was sweeping the downstairs bar and felt a tapping on my shoulders. I turned around and nobody was behind me. Of course I heard no one sneaking up because there were bottle caps on the floor. On another night, one of the bouncers was stocking the coolers when the light went out. He took the light from the hall and it worked in the cooler. Took the cooler light, it worked in the hall; switched them again, it didn't work. Keep in mind there's no way to shut the cooler light off. He started to put the beer away and someone tapped him on the shoulder. He never ran so fast."

Haunted Castle (former)
Archer & Western Avenues
Chicago, IL.

One of Brighton Park's most beautiful mansions once stood on the southwest corner of Archer and Western Avenues. This residence, surrounded by trees, shrubbery and flowers, was owned by a doctor. When he died, his will contained a clause stating that the mansion should stand as long as possible. No relatives were found and the mounting taxes eventually equaled the value of the building.

In its decline, the mansion was known as the "Haunted Castle." In spite of lack of upkeep, the shrubbery, flowers and trees always bloomed as before. The state finally sold the property, but the building was so dilapidated that it had to be torn down. Many local residents still have souvenirs they found in the noted mansion when it was being wrecked.

"Haunted Palace" (former)
Taylor & Sholto Streets
Chicago, IL.

Around 1901 a house on the West Side was known as the "haunted palace." Surrounded by decayed frame cottages, this imposing stone building would have attracted attention without the remarkable stories that were reported about it for a generation.

In 1873 Peter Fanning, a wealthy stonecutter, thought the neighborhood would someday become the fashionable residence of the West Side. Real estate in that section was booming and Fanning was one of the first to step in and purchase the corner lot on Taylor and Sholto Streets.

Then he started construction on a house of his own ideas. Among his acquaintances, "Old Man Fanning" was considered odd. He first startled the neighbors by the massive stone foundation he laid for his house. This reaction was mild to the one produced when he erected a high stone wall around his property and proceeded to decorate it with the most grotesque images carved in stone. Massive iron gates were cemented in the wall, and after the lawn was laid out, Fanning employed all his arts as a stonecutter to originate unheard of designs in stone carvings to decorate his yard. Chinese devils, imps, and weird and wonderful things from the sea were strewn about the lawn in insane fashion, and all this time Fanning, with a few trusted workmen, worked mysteriously on the wonderful foundation of his house. An immense iron vault with secret chambers and hidden entrances was, it was claimed, built in the solid masonry, and Fanning intimated to his friends that in this iron box, he would place his wealth. No one was allowed inside Fanning's high stone wall, and when not personally superintending the work of his vault he stood guard at the heavy iron gates to discourage the curious.

Just as the foundation was completed, Fanning suddenly died and work was stopped on the place. The two Fanning daughters did not care to finish the task started by their eccentric father, and Peter Fanning's stonework remained for years as he left it.

It wasn't long after the old man's death, that neighbors returning home late at night declared they saw Fanning's ghost roaming around the deserted ruins. Many believed the old man had deposited vast treasures in the hidden vault and had returned to guard his gold. Others claimed the restless spirit could not find the secret entrance and a party of the neighbors was organized to assist the ghost in hunting for the treasure. Every night the ghost of old Fanning haunted the ruins and during the day the neighbors joined in the search. Scores of people firmly believed they saw the old man's spirit nightly among the ruins and so persistent were they that few would walk by the spot at night. Little school children gazed with awe through the big iron gates and were frightened away by the rustle of a leaf.

The ground increased in value but the neighborhood was not the fashionable residence district that Fanning had pictured. It became, in fact, the haunt of Chris Merry and men of his type. At last Fanning's daughters, Mary and Anna decided to finish the house and live in it.

Instead of following their father's plan, they placed an upper structure of cheap material on the expensive foundation and removed as many of the weird carvings as possible. They moved into the place, but still the neighbors swore the ghost haunted the basement and cast a "hoodoo" on the clapboard store that was erected on the beautiful lawn facing on Sholto Street. Whatever doubts were cast on the ghost theory, the fact remained that the corner brought bad luck. All the businesses without exception failed. A tenant seldom remained more than a month before he realized the truth of the rumor.

Frank Garrity in 1898 was the last tenant to brave the ghost and when he opened his saloon he announced that he had come to stay. However, the "free lunch" he had prepared for his "grand opening" disappeared from his bolted kitchen without a trace. Garrity, like his predecessors, was compelled to acknowledge a supernatural influence.

The two Fanning sisters moved away one night and were never seen again. From then on the "To Rent" sign hung on the property until it was razed by the wreckers.

Metro
3730 N. Clark St.
Chicago, IL. 60613
773-549-0203

Formerly known as the Cabaret Metro, this music club has dropped the cabaret nonsense, but has retained its format and its reputation ac Chicago's premiere alternative rock stage; featuring breaking progressive bands of several genres. The Metro has a large stage, a good PA, room for about 1,100 people and a rococo ceiling to boot. A theater at one time, now with the seating removed. This was the starting point for Smashing Pumpkins, Ministry and many others. Apparently the upper floor is the scene of multiple haunting reports.

Many incidents in the ladies restroom have been reported by patrons to the club including suffocation attempts by hands unseen. This happens most often to single females alone in the upstairs restroom and is quite disquieting. Misty forms have also been seen too, very indistinct, but definitely something resembling a human-like figure.

When the place shuts down for clean-up, employees often hear strange, unexplained voices and sounds drifting down from the upstairs even though no one is up there. A lot of unexplained mysteries going on here. This place needs additional research.

Elizabeth McCarthy House
Formerly at 35th & Cottage Grove
Chicago, IL. 60653

For many years an old mansion stood at 35th and Cottage Grove Avenue which the owner offered rent free to anyone who would live in it. No renter was ever found for with the generous offer came the agreement that one room must forever remain locked and its mystery never penetrated.

This property at one time was among the finest in the city. Elizabeth McCarthy built it not long after the Great Chicago Fire of 1871 in the style of that time. Standing on the edge of town, the big lawns and grove of trees made the place a landmark.

The turn of the century, however, found it in ruins. The old mansion slowly tumbled down, weeds covered the pretty lawn and huge lilac bushes partly hid the house from view. The grounds which reached back to Vincennes Avenue were filled with debris and the fence facing on Cottage Grove Avenue fell into decay.

In the decade following the fire old Mrs. McCarthy had been a character in the neighborhood. For years she suffered with rheumatism, and at any time of day of night could be seen sitting in her room looking down Cottage Grove Avenue.

It was this room that her three daughters who inherited the house wanted kept "just as mother left it," and they insisted that the house be occupied only under these conditions. This room was the only one that remained furnished in the old mansion and from this fact stories crept out that the house was haunted.

People returning late at night declared that they saw the ghostlike face of Mrs. McCarthy in the window and that occasionally her spirit roamed out among the lilac bushes only to disappear behind the old trees in the rear of the grounds.

From time to time some hardy soul, attracted by the prospect of free rent, would be lured into entering the old house, which had long been turned over to scampering rats. The wooden floors would creak as the hesitant renter tread over them and the rotting porches menaced every step. The stairs leading to the mysterious room had fallen through. The lock to the door was nearly rusted away and only a thin piece of iron kept anyone from walking into the mysterious room. But no house hunter ever did. At this point he would depart in haste, unwilling to consider it at any price.

An old lady who once lived in Hyde Park told how one afternoon, many years ago, she and her brothers took a dare to gaze through a broken shutter.

In the room so long occupied by Mrs. McCarthy, the old furniture stood in its accustomed place, only a thick covering of mold showing the time that had elapsed since it was last used. Mrs. McCarthy's bed was in the same condition in which she left it and on the table were strewn musty books. An old pair of crutches, the owner's constant companions, stood by the bed just where she placed them, and the lamp with its oil gone made a support for a high spider web fashioned from the wall. The spider was the only living creature to share the room with the rats which scurried away at the first noise the children made.

The old rocking chair in which the ghost of the deserted mansion was said to sit kept silent sentinel by the window. Even though the children saw no ghost, nothing could induce them to pass beyond the gate leading to the yard again, not even the lilacs that bloomed in the spring and the sweet clover that ripened in the fall on the untended lawns.

The sign "Private Grounds - No Trespassing under Penalty" was unnecessary. For a generation neighbors gave the place a wide berth at night and were satisfied by day to gaze through the rails of the fence at the mansion where Mrs. McCarthy's ghost was never disturbed.

Music Box Theatre
3733 N. Southport Ave.
Chicago, IL. 60613
773-871-6604

The Music Box Theatre's history is similar to that of other neighborhood movie theaters throughout the city of Chicago with the exception that is was the first small interpretation of a "Movie Palace". It opened on August 22, 1929 as an elaborate little brother to the giant downtown film/presentation houses. It featured second-run films after they left the downtown for the neighborhood circuits. In its declining years, it slipped into a sleazy $1.50 grind house policy showing last year films. The last Hollywood film to play here was "The Exorcist" in the fall of 1977.

The house was built for a cost (including the seats) of about $110,000.00. The entire building, which includes the theater, nine storefronts and 32 apartments, cost about $260,000.00 according to an article in the August 1929 edition of Theatre Architecture Magazine. Theater equipment, exclusive of seats, was noted as $35,000. The architect was Louis A. Simon, a local, supposedly eccentric architect who was better known for his depression era W.P.A. Post Offices and plaster palaces for the avant garde nouveau riche. The building was erected by The Southport Avenue Businessmen's Association and operated by Lasker & Sons, which operated several smaller neighborhood houses in Chicago.

As Chicago Tribune Architectural Critic, Paul Gapp wrote (Arts and Books, July 31, 1983), "The architectural style is an eclectic mélange of Italian, Spanish and Pardon-My-Fantasy put together with passion." The actual style is called "atmospheric". The dark blue cove lit ceiling with "twinkling stars" and moving cloud formations suggests a night sky. The plaster ornamentation of the side walls, round towers, faux-marble loggia and ogee-arched organ chambers are, by Hollywood standards, reminiscent of the walls surrounding an Italian courtyard. Overall the effect is to make the patron feel that, no matter what the real weather outside; they are watching a film in an open air Palazzo where the evening temperature is always a balmy 72 degrees.

The theater opened in 1929 with Morton Downey (Sr.) in Mother's Boy. First-run film distribution in the 1930s thru '50s was in the hands of the studio owned downtown movie palaces. In 1983, the current operators leased the closed theater. It had been used sporadically between 1977 and 1983 for Spanish language films, porno films and lastly, Arabic language films. After an arduous four month restoration, the theater reopened in August of 1983. The presentation format was revival and repertory films in double features. The opening features were "Wabash Ave." with Betty Grable and Victor Mature and "In Old Chicago" with Alice Faye, Don Ameche and Tyron Power.

Within eight years, cult films, independent films and documentaries were added for a one week playtime intermingled with double feature repertory. First-run foreign films were added to the roster in 1986. The Music Box Theatre now presents a yearly average of 300 films making it Chicago's year-round film festival.

Old theaters have ghosts and The Music Box is no exception. It has its resident caretaker. "Whitey", as was his neighborhood nick-name, was the manager of The Music Box from opening night in 1929 to November 24, 1977. His wife was the cashier and they raised their family two blocks away from the theater.

According to one of Whitey's daughters, he spent most of his time at the theater. Young people who grew up in the neighborhood tell tales of working for Whitey, being tossed out by Whitey and accidentally-on-purpose skinning their knee to get a free piece of candy from Whitey.

Parents speak of the embarrassment of having their child's instamatic photo in the cashier' station "rogues gallery" of children not allowed back in the theater for any of a myriad of offenses.

On Thanksgiving eve, 1977, Whitey returned to close the theater. He fell asleep on the couch in the lobby and never woke up. The theater closed.

Whitey is a tireless protector of The Music Box Theatre. He helps solve problems and has been known to express his opinion of a bad organist by causing the drapery to drop in both organ chambers simultaneously. He is a very positive contributor to the audience comfort and enjoyment of his theater. He is Manager Emeritus.

Old Robey Tavern (former)
Washington & Damen Avenues
Chicago, IL.

West Side superstition accredits a quiet ladylike black-robed ghost to one of the corners of Washington Boulevard and Robey Street (now Damen Avenue). Its habitation was the old house known years ago as Robey's Tavern, at which time it stood in the center of an 800-acre farm several miles from town.

In those days the tavern was the gathering place of farmers, driving their slow-going ox-teams. Traders of all kinds made it headquarters, and somewhere out of this dim past the ghost lady who is supposed to walk these premises at night is supposed to have come. She has been described by several persons who have seen her as wearing a black gown with short waist, and with sleeves in the French style of 1800. She wears a large collar and cuffs, all of finest lace. She is supposed to be the disembodied spirit of the first Mrs. Robey. The Perkins family, who once occupied the house back around the turn of the century, had not seen the wraith. The story is all in the mouths of others, who have seen the figure walking noiselessly with folded hands.

The house in which this figure was said to walk originally was of wood. It was later raised on a brick foundation fourteen feet high. It was repainted and looked quite as modern as the ordinary houses built before the great fire.

It is said that the first "hanging" bee in Cook County assembled in front of this old farm house and that the body of the man swung from the limbs of a big tree in front of it.

Later a resident, who is a descendant of Alexander Hamilton and a relation of Abraham Lincoln, had not been disturbed by the black-robed shadow which others say they have seen in the house.

Red Light Restaurant
820 W. Randolph St.
Chicago, IL. 60607
312-733-8880

Named best new restaurant in 1997 by Esquire Magazine, Chicago's Red Light is the little sister to hot spots Marche and Gioco. Located in Chicago's West Loop, also known as the Randolph Street Market District, Red Light offers a traditional Chinese, Thai, Malaysian and partly Vietnamese menu concentrating on vegetarian and seafood cooking while having the flexibility to respect and honor the dietary preferences of today's Chicago diner.

Red Light is hard to miss. A 22-foot steel and fiberglass light towers above the entrance and acts as the larger-than-life sign for the restaurant and large windows encased in a hand-crafted steel and wood frame allow passerby to catch a glimpse of the Red Light scene. Inside the restaurant, wave shaped ribs climb up the walls and move across the undulating ceiling, ultimately flowing into the dramatic single-file open kitchen, signature design element of owner/designer Jerry Kleiner.

Opened in September of 1996, and previously a florist, one would never guess what its previous function was. Transformed into a spacious restaurant with black walnut flooring with a vintage wooden bar, most patrons have no idea anything strange or paranormal has been reported here in the past.

A former manager would often complain of hearing her named called while walking into the dining room, most times during peak hours, and not late at night or before closing. She would invariably turn around only to find no one there, of course, and it's happened to others as well.

The ever-present "door opening with no one around" happens here quite a bit or would become locked when no employees were present who had a key to do so. Near the old wooden bar electrical disturbances are frequent including the bar lights that dim and brighten with no corporeal person nearby.

During its first few years, Red Light was quite active but since 2000, it's been very quiet and tranquil. Perhaps the ghost was, at first, upset with the change but now quite pleased with the current incarnation of the building? Only time will time.

Rockwell Street Ghost
Rockwell Street & Humboldt Blvd.
Chicago, IL.

Out in the northwestern part of the city a house that remained vacant for years because everyone in the neighborhood believed it haunted was, in 1936, occupied by a family who declared the erstwhile ghost has forsaken its haunt.

The ghosts who flitted about the ancient house and terrified the neighbors proved on investigation to be members of a juvenile "gang" who had made a clubroom of the deserted house for several years.

The structure once stood at the southwest corner of Rockwell Street and Humboldt Boulevard was for years alone on the edge of town. There were no other buildings near, the street was poorly lighted, and when the icy winds swept the prairie, the occupants moved out, giving as a reason the fact that the place was too lonesome and remote.

One night the nearest neighbors were startled by mysterious lights which flickered in the windows of the deserted house. The report was promptly started that the place was haunted and after that no one would go within hailing distance of the house after dark. Even the policeman on the beat looked with suspicion on the place, and in making his lonely rounds walked on the opposite side of the street. Every night lights were seen in the windows and some alleged that ghostly shadows accompanied them.

Gradually the neighborhood was built up, and in time the "haunted house" was surrounded with bungalows and small homes. One night the police organized a party, and armed with revolvers and clubs, invaded the place. The boys who had secretly dubbed themselves the "Spook Club" were discovered in a game of poker.

That settled the fate of the ghosts. The house was cleaned up and soon rented. The ghosts grew up and became fathers. Over poker games they would often chuckle over their boyhood joke in the "haunted house."

Thurston's
Formerly at 1248 W. George St.
Chicago, IL. 60657
773-472-6900

Thurston's showcases the best of Chicago's local talent. Bands take to the stage upstairs; or take in the funky decor and a few mixers on the first floor. Menu items include pizza and calzones.

This site once housed a slaughterhouse where animals were killed and prepared for market. Thurston's was allegedly haunted by the spirits of those animals butchered on the site. That is until owner, Mark Romano, called upon the services of a local priest to bless the building and contents inside. Since then, according to most, the cleansing technique was successful. Employees claim to have had no current experiences there since the priest did his thing. Perhaps it worked? Maybe the animal's ghosts are only lying dormant waiting to be again awoken.

The location has closed down and is not open to the public at last visit.

NORTH SIDE HAUNTS

Barat College
700 E. Westleigh Rd.
Lake Forest, IL. 60045
847-234-3000

Barat traces its origin to 19th century France and St. Madeleine Sophie Barat, who founded the Society of the Sacred Heart in 1800. The model of Sacred Heart education was unique in its time because of its commitment to rigorous, values-based, formal education for women with the expectation that these women would assume responsibility for influence and leadership in their families and in the world. Since 1800 the Society of the Sacred Heart has established a large number of schools, colleges and other works in forty-four countries and six continents. St. Rose Philippine Duchesne established the Society of the Sacred Heart in the United States in 1818. Philippine opened the first school of the Sacred Heart in St. Charles, Missouri.

Barat College began as an academy for young women in Chicago in 1858. The school moved to its Lake Forest location in 1904. In 1918, the State of Illinois chartered Barat as a four-year college, Governance of the College passed from the Society of the

Sacred Heart to an independent Board of Trustees in 1969. The college exists independent of financial support from the Roman Catholic Church.

Barat followed its physical growth by expanding its educational reach in the 1970s by including adult re-entry students. In 1982, Barat College became a co-educational institution. Through all these significant changes, the school has maintained the founding vision of St. Madeleine Sophie Barat to offer a highly personalized education tailored to each student's strengths while caring for the intellectual and spiritual well-being of the total person.

To ensure long-term growth and increased educational opportunities for all students, Barat College formed an educational alliance with DePaul University in February 2001.

The haunting appears confined to the chapel within the Old Main Building, a Georgian Revival motif, which also houses some faculty and administration offices as well as most of the classrooms. An olfactory experience is sometimes encountered by those passing through the chapel at various times of the day and night.

The smell is thought to be that of flowers or even candles that seems to be confined to a corridor along side the chapel and no where else. A true "psychic scent" it is only present in a very small exact area and does not slowly dissipate when you walk away from the odor. The scent is extremely strong when encountered and when you take a few steps away, suddenly it's entirely gone! It doesn't become less and less noticeable, but drops off at once. The scent is sometimes thought to be roses and roses are the most often encountered psychic floral scent. The grave of Mary Alice Quinn in Holy Sepulchre Cemetery in Worth, Illinois and Julia Buccola Peta's grave in Mount Carmel Cemetery located in Hillside, Illinois are prime examples of the psychic rose scent that has been sniffed for years even in the dead of winter. (See Windy City Ghosts)

A possible explanation was researched by a student who talked to a nun that had been there for many years. The sister told her that there was a long-standing tradition which supposedly began in the 1930s called a Daisy Chain Ceremony in which chains of daisies mixed with ferns were carried thru the corridors and right up to the Sacred Heart Statue. The upperclassmen would form a circle around the statue and the seniors would symbolically pass the chain to their lower class men. Roses and candles were also used in the ceremony which would explain the psychic smells still present today.

Dole Mansion
401 Country Club Rd.
Crystal Lake, IL. 60014
815-459-7286

On February 18, 1836, Beman and Polly Crandall built a log cabin, moved their six children in and stayed to have four more kids, and a simple, happy life. Their homestead was at the intersection of Van Buren and Virginia in what later became Crystal Lake. They were the first permanent settlers of the area. The first business district was about where the Dole Mansion, built in 1865, now stands. It consisted of a general store, a wagon shop, a shoe store, a blacksmith shop and a stage coach stop tavern on Virginia Avenue. The north side of town was another small village known as Nunda (pronounced "Nun-Day"). Later, in 1914, the two towns merged, and Crystal Lake, then a city, extended from the lake to the Fox River.

This mansion was originally owned and lived in by some of the area's most prominent families; many of them now reside in nearby Lake Avenue Cemetery. Recently, the First Congregational Church of Crystal Lake purchased it and is now protected by the Dole Mansion Preservation Society.

Stacy McArdle used to work there in the late 1980s and distinctly remembers the vacuum cleaner plug being pulled out of the socket while cleaning the oldest/original part of the building. Sometimes while fixing the beds, leaving the room for a moment, and returning with clean towels, she would find the bedcovers pulled back as though someone was preparing for sleep. Cold spots were often encountered by McArdle, even on the hottest of days.

Her boyfriend, at the time, sometimes heard strange knocking sounds on various windows from the outside of the pane while he was washing them! On one occasion the sounds actually followed him down the banister of one hallway.

An article in the Northwest Herald, dated October 26, 1997 reads: "Bob Donelli doesn't scare easily. But he couldn't help feeling paranoid after moving into his Crystal Lake home in 1992. Almost immediately, he started sensing a presence in the house. 'You could feel it anywhere,' said Donelli, a meat cutter. 'It's like, you weren't alone.' The house, reportedly once located on the Dole Mansion estate had housed workers from an ice company. Donelli never investigated to find out if this 'presence' was a ghost. And he never looked into the history of the home. It finally left in 1995, but he knows what it felt like when it was there. 'Like an indefinable fear,' he said. "There have been no formal investigations of the Dole Mansion because current owners claim it isn't haunted by anything.

Duncan Avenue
Fox River near East Dundee, IL.

Apparitions have been reported by people traveling on Duncan Avenue near the Fox River. These apparitions were reported by Horacio Minjares, a Carpentersville tradesman and civic booster, who heard them from his daughters and friends. His report is as follows:

"They are on Duncan near the bike path footbridge (under I-90). They are ghostly apparitions but very clear. At first you think that they are people because they appear to be solid, but when you look at them again, you realize there is a lack of color.

"The experience lasts for about four seconds. At the end of the experience they (witnesses) have to stop and throw up because of the intense emotional experience. Mostly it's been young people who have told me about it. I was skeptical but when my daughters saw them, I thought otherwise. They said they saw a woman in a lime green dress on, and although there usually is a lack of color, sometimes there is maybe a suggestion of color.

"This woman had a lime dress on, and they also described a feeling of intense sorrow and loneliness, but no fear. The apparitions are by the side of the road and in the woods there. I've heard numbers ranging from seven to eight people and up to 40 and 50 at one time.

"I first heard about it in November. Then I heard another story in the middle of December, and the girls experienced something in the first week of January. This usually happens before midnight. Two other sets of young people, a boy and girl and two brothers, between 17 and 22, also reported them.

"The first thing I asked them was, 'What were you smoking and what's going on?' But my middle daughter, Itzel, is an unbeliever and tends to have a rationalist attitude where everything has to be explained logically, and she was completely taken aback. So I thought maybe there's something to this.

"The lady in green was short, 5 feet tall, short dark wavy hair, she looks Latina. They were driving by when they saw this. They said they experienced a strange feeling and then there were people on both sides."

Itzel herself described the apparition as strange, but not scary.

"At first I wasn't sure what it was, but it gave me bad feeling and I knew it was something bad," said Itzel. "There were a lot of people. It was weird. It wasn't scary. I was with my older sister and she wanted to go back, but I wouldn't go back. The lady was standing on the east side of the road.

"It was very sad. The people we saw didn't look scary. They looked sad. That's what we both felt. We both felt really sick. I couldn't even talk. We felt sick like we wanted to throw up. We used to travel on that road often, but not anymore."

There doesn't seem to be any history to explain these strange occurrences at present.

Elmhurst Public Library
211 Prospect Ave.
Elmhurst, IL. 60126
630-279-8696

In 1868, Seth Wadhams would build a home for his family, White Birch, which eventually was to become the Elmhurst Public Library. In 1887, it became the summer home of the Henry W. King family. A year later, Mr. King constructed a large, two-story addition on the north side with a vast porch. From 1906 to 1921, it belonged to Thomas E. Wilder, then known at Lancaster Lodge. Finally, the library moved in 1922 on the first floor of the Wilder home which had been purchased, along with an acre of land, from the park district for $14,000.

In 1930, a fire damaged the north roof. Later, in that year the building was rewired, redecorated and part of the second floor was remodeled for library use. Almost constant remodeling and expanding took place right up to the present. In 2003, Elmhurst Public Library will move to a much larger, modern and up-to-date facility.

Of course, all this remodeling does sometimes have its setbacks, especially if there is a ghost present. Spirits often become disturbed and feisty if their surroundings are changed or altered in anyway. Such appears to be the case at the Elmhurst Library. Both employees and library-goers have reported "poltergeist" activity within, including books that fly off shelves or, the opposite, books re-shelving themselves. I know the library staff appreciates the latter.

Other phenomena include lights being discovered still on by employees in the morning when the library is being prepared for opening to the public and the constant feeling of being watched and/or followed by unseen presences.

Some believe that the ghost is none other then ol' Seth Wadham, himself and that he was something perturbed of the constant changes to his homestead. With each new remodeling, more phenomena were alleged to have taken place within the confines. Eventually some library staff resigned themselves to the fact that the place might indeed be haunted.

With the eventual move to the new building in a few years, perhaps Wadham can finally rest in peace with the promise of no new major structural changes. But I guess that depends on who will eventually purchase the grand old house.

The First Methodist Church of Evanston
516 Church St.
Evanston, IL. 60201
847-864-6181

The sanctuary of this grand church is haunted by the ghost of a man in a black business suit. It is within this sanctuary that the oldest object of the church resides; a 15th century French Gothic clergy stall with elaborate carvings. Nearby, panels of wood carved reredos depict scenes from the life of Jesus. All the stained glass windows in the nave were designed and built in London and installed in 1930. These windows include the Frances Willard likeness, the John Wesley window and Te Deum window.

This ghostly figure, dressed quite appropriately for church, walks down the side aisle of the sanctuary, coming out from behind one pillar and walking behind the next. However, if you look behind that pillar, no one will be there! There are no doors or windows that he could have gone through.

It is unknown who he is or why he is haunting the church.

Galena History Museum
211 S. Bench Street
Galena, IL. 61036
815-777-9129

    The Galena/Jo Daviess County Historical Society and Museum is a private, non-profit organization founded in 1938 to collect preserve and interpret the history of Galena and Jo Daviess County, Illinois. All housed in an 1858 beautiful Italianate home built as a private residence by Galena merchant Daniel Barrows. Constructed on the site of a home previously destroyed by fire, he owned a distillery, a confectionery store and later, a lumber yard. Barrows pretty much lost everything he owned just after the conclusion of the Civil War. He had to give up his beautiful mansion just shortly after his wife died.

    Families continued to live in this home until 1922 when the Odd Fellows Lodge bought it. After making some extensive renovations including the removal of a rear wing and building a large two-story hall in its place, they sold the property to the City of Galena in 1938. City Hall was housed in the front two rooms of the building and a museum association took over the remaining space with a 99 year lease. In 1967, the city vacated the premises and left the structure for historical society use.

    The first sign of some paranormal activity was reported in the spring of 1989. Footsteps were heard and employees began to record the events on a computer file. Shuffling of feet and the footsteps continued and were a constant occurrence. At first employees thought the sounds might have been either birds, rodents, plaster falling from the ceiling or possibly even a hoaxster.

    The piano located in a large hall would often sound a single chord without the assistance of human hands. Others reported hearing the sounds of footsteps sometimes passing right by them while ascending or descending the stairs. Sounds of furniture being rearranged on the top floor were reported on several occasions. When they would go upstairs to investigate, there would be nothing amiss! No chairs or other furnishings were moved or displaced.

    Chandeliers would swing without any breeze present in one of the offices of the establishment. Floor boards would constantly creak and moan as if someone were walking around. According to long-time employees, the floors only make a noise when someone is walking on them. In other words, the house has long since settled.

    In January of 1991 during a convention held at the site for VIPs, a waitress dropped an entire tray of champagne on the floor making quite a mess. Approximately ten minutes later another server observed the filled glasses on the tray begin to tremble and shake. Before she knew it, the glasses and tray also fell to the floor. Both were reprimanded and told to be more careful by the person in charge. About this time, another person saw 8-10 glasses sitting on a tray not being held by anyone also begin to shake violently. Before anyone could reach the tray to prevent another mishap, almost half of them also tumbled to the floor. This happened one more time to another server.

About 40 years ago, former Mayor Logan, while holding a city council meeting in the building when it was still City Hall, began to hear such a loud commotion in the upstairs hallway that they all left to investigate the source of the sounds. By the time they all arrival at the hallway, all was silent.

Many believe that the ghost is none other than the original owner Daniel Barrows who may be unhappy because of the structural changes made to the house by the Odd Fellows Lodge or the subsequent owners treatment of the house in general. Often when renovations or extreme structural changes are made to an abode, this seems to infuriate the resident ghost. They like to remember the house as it was while they were alive and living within. Or perhaps, the ghost just didn't care much for the taste of champagne.

Greenwood Cemetery
Greenwood Road
Woodstock, IL. 60098

Pennsylvania investor and financier, Henry King purchased the property that would later become Greenwood Cemetery in 1840. The first official burial here was that of Elbridge Boone in 1838 and whose father resided on the property a few years before it was purchased by King. The most famous burial here is said to be Ann McQuinn. She arrived here around 1833 which would have made her the first white woman to live in the county.

Graves of Civil War veterans are represented here as well as the victim of a very brutal murder.

A number of local area researchers including Stacy McArdle, have captured strange mists and globes (orbs) on film on numerous occasions. There has been EVP (Electronic Voice Phenomena), voices of the dead, recorded here in the past.

One researcher, a number of years ago, had an unusual experience with a friend who tagged along to visit the site. A high-pitched scream which seemed to emanate from the center of the cemetery was heard by both. According to the couple, they had been there for well over an hour and they hadn't seen anyone else in the vicinity. The sound wasn't an animal because they described it as "too human."

Holcombville School
Crystal Lake, IL. 60014

Holcombville School is a tiny one-room dilapidated building held together today with steel harnesses which was built circa 1858 and was designated a landmark by the McHenry Preservation Committee in 1995.

This petite structure is apparently haunted by students of long ago as visitors to the site have often heard a strange tapping on the windows from the inside as they peer through the dirty panes. One local resident allegedly used an Ouija Board with a friend at the front of the building in 1990. According the report, the planchette began moving around the board without their hands touching it, just as they began to hear some sounds reverberating from within. A few minutes later, they fled the area when they heard the distinct sound of a bell overheard but could not locate. They claimed to have even felt the vibrations in their ears.

The school has been closed for years and isn't very safe to enter, even if permission were given. Tape recorders should prove to be an interesting test of EVP, if one could gain entry to the building.

Hooters Restaurant
660 N. Wells Street
Chicago, IL. 60610
312-944-8800

Hooter's of America, Inc. is the Atlanta-based operator and franchiser of over 250 Hooters locations in 40 states. The first Hooters opened October 2, 1983 in Clearwater, Florida by the infamous Hooters six and their company Hooters Inc., the founders of the Hooters trademark. Hooters was the fasting growing restaurant chain in 1991 and 1992. Even though most think of *Married With Children* and Al Bundy when they think of Hooters, cooperate bosses point to their owl logo as the theme for their restaurant chain.

Chicago's Hooters is built along the edge of Ontario and Clark Streets nightlife where a number of other popular night spots are also located including the Hard Rock Café, Excalibur, the Rain Forest Café and the Rock 'N Roll McDonalds. However, a number of other prominent businesses have failed while these have thrived. Could it be due to the Great Chicago Fire of 1871 which ravaged through this area killing many people? Or are there other unexplainable reasons?

Bartenders have claimed to have experienced quite a few ghostly episodes while working in the restaurant including hearing their names called and having the sensation of someone touching them on the shoulder. Of course, when they turn around, no one is present. This often occurs in the storage room in the basement of Hooters. Others have heard the sounds of running feet, chasing after them as they descend the steps to the basement storage. Again, no flesh and blood person can account for the noises.

The phones have acted quite peculiar including all three lines ringing in unison, only to discover that no one was on any of the lines at the time. Ameritech was called to investigate for a possible malfunction but found none.

Jukeboxes display a mind of their own, coming on for no apparent reason and other electrical appliances have been affected as well. This seems to follow a typical pattern of ghosts having an affinity for electricity and electrical objects. Perhaps their own electrical frequencies simply interfere with the normal frequencies in these devices? Or perhaps they are just trying to show employees that they are indeed around.

Kennicot House
1421 Milwaukee Avenue
Glenview, IL. 60025
847-299-6069

Kennicot House was built in 1856 by Dr. John A. Kennicot a prominent Illinois physician, horticulturist and educational and agricultural leader. Kennicot moved to "The Grove" as it's also known from New Orleans in 1836, shortly after the birth of his son Robert. In 1835, he devoted much of his time to the study and promotion of horticulture and agriculture, developing The Grove into the first major nursery in northern Illinois. Robert Kennicot developed an interest in nature at an early age, studying with his father. He helped found the Chicago Academy of Sciences, and his explorations of Alaska gave the United States its first scientific knowledge of that region and influenced the decision for its purchase.

Kennicot House allegedly is haunted by a headless body of a woman who appears to be walking down the front staircase. She is dressed in the style of the 1800s; the same period as when the family lived in the home. A light, as if from an oil lamp, is seen moving about the house. When police have gone to investigate, there is no one there and no sign of forced entry. Although, allegedly, it was on one such call that the police saw the headless apparition.

Lake Avenue Cemetery
Crystal Lake, IL. 60014

History is sketchy concerning this cemetery with the exception of the Dole's being buried within. Most of the grave markers date back to the late 1800s and located deep within a purely residential area, no activity was reported until the late 1980s. Allegedly an 18-year-old girl died on the cemetery property. Neighbors were horrified when they observed the woman apparently on fire and rolling around on the grass in an attempt to extinguish the flames.

According to police reports, she supposedly doused herself with lighter fluid and set herself on fire for reasons unknown.

Ever since that gruesome event, a horrible stench of burnt flesh has been encountered at various times of the day and night as you walk along the sidewalk with fronts the cemetery. Mysterious globes of light have been observed bouncing around the cemetery recently by both local residents and passerby.

Local researcher, Stacy McArdle, has, in her possession a picture of the alleged apparition which appears to be humanoid in configuration but made up of numerous balls of lights. A most unusual picture indeed. A most unusual haunting!

Mt. Thabor Cemetery
Mt. Thabor Road & Route 176
Crystal Lake, IL. 60014

Mt. Thabor was founded around 1846 by Owen Dyer, an Irishman who settled in the area. He deeded one acre of the land to the Catholic Church for $1, and for this, a log cabin was constructed on the property. It was called North Barrens Church and also Little Church in the Woods.

For awhile Mt. Thabor housed the only Catholic Church in the entire southwest section of the county. Some of the earliest families are interred here. There are graves that contain both Civil War and Mexican War veterans. According to cemetery records, there were close to 120 burials here, however only about 35 or so stones still remain standing today. No one is buried here today but in the 1960s a number of infants and children were buried in a large section of the property. Most of those buried in Mt. Thabor, however, date back to the 1890s or earlier.

Located in a very rural section of Crystal Lake, this cemetery is haunted by a number of various types of phenomena. The area is especially photogenic as many have come away with interesting pictures. In the late 1980s a woman apparently photographed what she described as a "phantom tombstone". Looking at the picture, you could almost read the inscription on the stone but at the same time, grass can be seen through the grave marker!

A number of orbs and green mists have been both seen and photographed and even GRS members on a trip to the site in 1998 photographed a nice round orb near a tombstone with a Polaroid camera. Voices of both genders have been heard sometimes laughing, sometimes singing or mumbling. Other times words can be ascertained. Most often a 'hello'. There has even been a whistling sound heard on occasion.

Green mists have been observed by many, orbs levitating around visitors to the site as well as around the baby plots. One time the entire center of the cemetery was brightly illuminated almost like daylight even though there was nothing that could have caused this naturally. There have been malfunctions caused to automobiles left running near the cemetery. Automobiles that are new and have no true mechanical problems.

GRS member John Cachel visited the cemetery in early November of 1998:

"On November 7, 1998, Walter Meyers and I went to Mt. Thabor Cemetery at night near Crystal Lake in northern Illinois. We noticed a scent that we agreed is women's strong perfume. It was near a baby lot. We didn't wear any aftershave. There are no flowers, or anybody in the cemetery, just the two of us. We also smelled the same perfume at the north section of the cemetery. Maybe that's the same woman, who followed us. Who knows?

"We used Raytec infrared temperature scanner and we found a cold spot near a baby lot. It was 5 to 7 degrees from around 34 degrees so we followed the cold spot to the near northeast section of the cemetery where we lost it. We also found several cold spots as cold as about 32 to 34 degrees. We checked our scanner to the sky, (cloudy, about 45 degrees from the horizon). It read between 22 to 25 degrees so we knew that the temperature between 5 to 13 degrees on the horizon was something.

"I took three rolls of Kodak Goldmax (ASA 800) film and we found on several photos balls of light, a ghostly mist that spread across the entire frame of the photo and also several more solid shapes in the mist."

John made another trip to the cemetery in April of 1999:

"Last Friday my friend and I went to Mt. Thabor Cemetery at night. Not much happened, just a few orbs and one orange strand out of two rolls of film. I got several orbs and a faint cloudy (possible could be a mist if it's on photograph) from my Sony camcorder.

"Last Sunday I went there during the day to make maps. I also used my Sony camcorder for my records just in case. I noticed a small shadow about the size of a large butterfly that followed me. It took only about two seconds. About four to five seconds later, a white orb moved and curved to hit a large tombstone and went down to near the ground then floated away. I caught the orb's own shadow on the smaller tombstone."

This cemetery is surely one of the most haunted in the far northwestern suburbs and consistently produces interesting and often unexplainable spirit photographs.

Norwood Historical Society
5624 N. Newark Ave.
Chicago, IL. 60631
773-631-4633

There's nothing extraordinary about the history of Norwood Park. It was settled in 1833, by a farmer from Yorkshire, became a small farming community with its own rail depot and tavern, and was brought into the city in the 1890s, as Chicago was bulking up for the Columbian Exposition. But its first house, built by that same Yorkshire farmer, Mark Noble, is still standing, so the Norwood Park Historical has converted it into a museum.

In the early 20th Century, the house belonged to Stuart Crippen, a pianist who toured on the Chautauqua circuit, a more cultured version of vaudeville. One of the upstairs bedrooms has been decorated to look the way it did when Crippen's daughter was a young woman in the 1920s. There's a Singer sewing machine, a mirror, a comb, a tin of Outdoor Girl Face Powder and even a few pages from her diary are on display. A few years ago, someone swept the grounds of the house with a metal detector, and the findings are on display in another room: bottles, chinaware, nails, a lead soldier and coins dating back to 1854. The museum also has an old wooden pipe, part of Norwood Park's water system when it was still a village, and a wheel of lumber from what was reputed to be Norwood Park's oldest tree, a 150-year-old cottonwood felled in 1988.

Tony and Barbara are both die-hard historians and restorationists and devoted a lot of their spare time to restoring the aged Crippen house in the spring of 2000. Many times Tony would find himself completely alone in the large home. While copying important historical papers one afternoon, he distinctly heard a disembodied voice call out "Hey!" At first he thought he was probably the caretaker who had been working outside, but when peering out a window, it became apparent that the man was still outside playing with his dog a good distance away from the building. It couldn't have possibly been his voice that he just heard.

Putting that incident aside, he journeyed upstairs to retrieve some additional papers for photocopying when again he heard that same voice yell "Hey!" This time he thought that perhaps someone was playing tricks on him in the old house but he could find nobody nearby or anywhere in the house for that matter. The third time he heard the spectral yell, he was in the basement but ignored it and finished his work and departed the building.

Both Tony and Barbara are well accustomed to being or living in strange homes as they once resided in the boyhood home of mass murderer John Wayne Gacy on Marmora Avenue. They reportedly heard strange scraping sounds coming from the basement of that home from a chrome kitchen set. What was even more amazing is that the sounds continued after the set was trashed.

Perhaps the yells will continue or perhaps escalate when the massive restoration project gets into full swing. Only time will tell.

www.museumsusa.org/museums/info/1165417

Oakland Cemetery
Woodstock, IL. 60098

This rather large cemetery dates back to 1859. The graveyard is divided into different section or lots for pets, cremations, infants, American Legion veterans and even employees of Oliver Typewriter Company. At the end of the property is a big swampy marsh known as Choate's Pond and was once a very popular swimming spot for teenagers and adults alike. Sadness came to that pond in the late 1800s when two or more children drowned and then it ceased to be such a joyous place to frequent.

A rather large mausoleum on the property with the name Buck inscribed on it appears to be the epicenter of much paranormal activity. A number of years ago village officials ordered the mausoleum bricked up due to frequent break-ins from local teenagers at night, some of which included the scattering of the deceased remains!

Because of this desecration, unearthly screams have emanated from the confines of the structure over the years. Eyewitnesses have observed psychic forms that did not have an earthly explanation. Included were glowing globes of light bouncing in front of a group of late night visitors in October of 1997. Others described seeing and photographing an orange-yellow fire further back into the depths of the graveyard. As they approached this "fire", it receded further back until it simply disappeared. Still others have described seeing a black shadow set low to the ground which apparently wasn't cast by any in the group that evening.

Phantom animals, namely jaguars have been seen in the area and reported to local police three or four times. All the reports claim these animals just vanish from sight.

O'Hare Hilton
O'Hare International Airport
Chicago, IL. 60605
773-686-8000

The O'Hare Hilton Hotel is a five minute walk to any terminal at O'Hare and boasts 858 rooms including an aerobic area, the newest Nautilus workout equipment, a dentist office and shopping on the premises. Amenities include two bars and two first-class restaurants, The Gaslight and Andiamo. The hotel was designed to be completely soundproof; a real must in one of the world's busiest airports! With its many rooms there does seem to be just one that a lot of people have felt uncomfortable in, couldn't sleep and sometimes asked to be moved to another room.

While employees would not discuss the exact room number, they did speculate that it had something to do with an apparent suicide by hanging that occurred there a number of years ago. The haunted room located very close to an elevator, ice and soda machine. Some thought that the noise given off by the machines was a possible cause of the alleged phenomena. However each of the hotel's ten floors is equipped exactly the same, so that possible explanation was ruled out. Despite this, until recently, tenants still complained of uneasiness in the room while sleeping.

Currently the staff has reported that all is now quiet and that there have been no complaints recently in the room. Perhaps the ghost is at last at rest?

http://www.hilton.com/en/hi/hotels/index.jhtml?ctyhocn=CHIOHHH

The Pale Horse
Galena, IL. 61036

This story was retrieved from the Daily Gazette of March 16, 1874:
"Galena has got the ghosts, in the most malignant form. The first well-developed case made its appearance at the residence of a gentleman on Bench Street, whose wife is temporarily elsewhere on a visit to her relatives. On Saturday last, our friend invited a courageous young man to share his bed during the night, as sleeping with his wife's nightdress had ceased to be a novelty. The 'son of David' consented, and after a perusal of the horrible experiences of a traveling agent, as recounted in Saturday's Gazette, followed by a lengthy conversation on ghosts in general, the two retired to their sleeping room in the third story of the house, having satisfactorily settled the question, in their own minds, at least, that the ghost business was a fraud of the very worst type. In the course of time, the two had ensconced themselves upon the bed rail, and without speaking a word to each other, were gradually falling into the arms of Morpheus, when they were aroused by a terrible clatter issuing, apparently, from the basement. The hair of these hitherto incredulous and courageous men began to elevate, until it stood on ends like quills upon a fretful porcupine. With trembling limbs and dismayed countenances, they emerged from under the bed clothes, and lighting a lamp, cautiously made their way down stairs, armed to the teeth with al the munitions of war the house afforded. Arriving at the basement, they discovered nothing, and were laughing over their momentary fright, when a like noise, though more terrific in its nature, was heard in the upper part of the house. If any of the readers of the Gazette have ever been in a like situation, they can sympathize with these two affrighted gentlemen, who were undecided as to whether it was best to call in the neighbors, bolt for the street or lay right down and die in their tracks. A brief council of war was held, however, and our friends concluded to fight it out on that line, if it took until the morning. Our informant tells us that the balance of the night was spent by these two affrighted males in oscillating between the upper and lower part of the house, in search of the origin of the supernatural demonstrations, and that the mystery is yet unsolved."

Tamerack
River Road
Mt. Prospect, IL. 60056

One of the most colorful and perhaps the most tragic gangsters and bootleggers was a man by the name of Roger Touhy (1898-1959), who was given the nickname of "Terrible Touhy." Touhy was framed by the Capone mob with the apparent connivance of a corrupt Cook County State's Attorney named Thomas Courtney, who made political hay out of this page-one conviction. In 1933, when the international con-man Jake "The Barber" Factor was on the verge of extradition back to England for a raft of stock swindles foisted on overseas investors in the 1920s, it was decided to arrange a bogus kidnapping with the help of Frank Nitti, boss of the Chicago mob, who inherited this job after Capone was sentenced to prison. Factor was "abducted" outside the Dells Roadhouse in suburban Morton Grove, Illinois, taken to a safe house until a phony ransom was paid and his release assure.

With the connivance of the Nitti gang, Factor had fingered Touhy as his abductor. Touhy was an independent gangster and bootlegger who operated in the northwestern portion of the Chicagoland area and would run beer up as far as the Wisconsin border. Touhy was having his area encroached upon by the Capone mob and this phony kidnapping charge was just what they needed to rid themselves of Touhy for a long time. He escaped several times from prison only to be recaptured quite quickly. While imprisoned, he wrote a book about himself entitled, "The Stolen Years" which was released in 1959, the same year he was released from prison.

Luck, however, continued to elude Touhy and within thirty days of his exodus, he was gunned down from shotgun blasts in front of a little hotdog stand. As he lay dying the former gangster muttered, "I've been expecting it. The bastards never forget."

His former home Tamerack in Mount Prospect is surrounded by large trees was used, in the summer months, as a boy's camp. An inn directly across the road was used by Elliot Ness to watch Touhy while he resided there. From the Touhy house and across the road was a secret tunnel that beer was brought through the tunnel to the other side of the street and then loaded into trucks for delivery.

Touhy certainly left this world in a tragic, violent fashion and if anyone was to be a little bitter or to be haunting a certain area, it would be Roger Touhy. The reports are that Touhy's ghost is quite active here at his home. The light bulbs would constantly go on and off. Phantom footsteps and knocks on doors can be heard. In fact, knocks coming in a series of threes are reported and when someone goes to answer the door, they find no one around. A number of years ago, one of Touhy's sons claimed that there was a hidden treasure buried in the forest preserve across the road from the house. Treasure-hunters with metal detectors are constantly looking for the loot until forest rangers interceded. Perhaps that's another reason his ghost is still around, protecting his stashed loot.

Turner Hall
115 S. Bench Street
Galena, IL. 61036
815-777-0720

Turner Hall was built in 1874 from native stone. The first owner was the Turner Society. C. Barner, president of the Sociale Turners was quoted as saying, "The building was erected to supply a long want felt in Galena, and is designed for the special use of the citizens of the city, without regard to politics, religion, or nationality, as well as for the entertainments of a respectable character."

Over the years, General Tom Thumb entertained in 1877, U.S. Grant spoke in 1880 and Theodore Roosevelt spoke in 1900. Turner Hall was gutted by fire in 1926 and rebuilt in the 1930s, as part of the WPA project. Today Turner Hall hosts concerts, plays, dances and receptions...all "of a respectable character."

A number of people have experienced the ghost or ghosts at Turner Hall including those who work for the Save Turner Hall Fund organization. Cold spots are frequently encountered within and are often described as "bone chilling." The icy spells are often reported near the back stone wall and two workers both felt the chill and saw a small stone suddenly come loose from the wall.

Shadows are sometimes seen walking past the dressing rooms. The images are fleeting and unrecognizable. When witnesses search the area looking for what they believe to be a real person, they find nothing! Other times lights turn themselves on or off without anyone being anywhere near the light switches.

A local Dubuque, Iowa psychic visited the theater a number of years ago and claimed that she saw a spirit in the balcony. This was most likely picked up clairvoyantly as others present could not see the specter.

Who could the ghost be? Charles Scheerer was the first manager of the theater and was part of the Scheerer, Armbruster and Coleman firm dealing in furniture and coffins! Their establishment was right next to the theater and they were often called upon for their services. On March 14, 1910, he was found dead in the theater, probably from natural causes. Perhaps he is still around looking after affairs, concerts and productions still produced in the building? Perhaps he just doesn't want to let go yet?

http://www.turnerhall.com/

Uptown Theater
4816 N. Broadway
Chicago, IL. 60640

The Uptown Theater, located just north of Lawrence Avenue on Broadway, was opened to the public in August of 1925. It was built by the famous Balaban & Katz circuit of movie palaces and joined the Tivoli, the Central Park, the Chicago and Uptown's own Riviera as part of that rapidly expanding chain. Designed by architects C.W. and George L. Rapp was loosely derived from Spanish Baroque architecture and included nearly 4,500 seats, making it the second largest movie palace in the United States after New York's radio City Music Hall.

Like all movie palaces of the 1910s and 1920s, the Uptown was conceived and designed by its owners as a way to legitimize and reap profits off a previously disreputable form of entertainment. Motion pictures, and the theaters in which they were shown, had been much maligned by social reformers during the 1910s. Chains like Balaban & Katz and theaters like the Uptown were meant to reverse this trend by presenting those same motion pictures in more "respectable" surroundings.

The architects of the theater, the well-known Rapp brothers, made sure that the theater's appearance would allay people's fears about the immorality of movie-going. Through their handiwork, the Uptown became one of the most spectacular structures on Chicago's North Side, complete with its elaborate Spanish Renaissance decor and its five-story chandeliered Grande lobby. Its monumentality was rivaled only by the area's largest churches. Other attractions at the $4-million theater included the most expensive Wurlitzer grand organ then to be built and a state-of-the-art air-conditioning system.

The theater was an overnight smash hit with the movie-going public and attracted large crowds even after attendance trailed off for other movie palaces during the late 1930s. Balaban & Katz liked to believe that their theaters enabled the masses to frequently enjoy the glamour of "legitimate" theater at an affordable price. Promoted as an "acre of seats in a magic city," the Uptown was no exception.

Phantom apparitions have been seen in the past by movie-goers, most often in the ladies' restroom situated in the basement of the theater. During the early 1970s, reports include an apparition of a man dressed in a black coat or cloak with a fedora-style hat on his head. However, no distinct facial features could be determined by the eyewitness at the time. It surely wasn't a real person, as the witness claimed that she saw no feet on the visage! This same figure was again observed by the same witness on another occasion in remarkably the same circumstances. It has also been observed by other employees including the manager's daughter on one occasion. Cold spots were also reported behind the screen on a staircase.

http://www.ci.chi.il.us/Landmarks/U/UptownTheater.html

William Fremd High School
1000 S. Quentin Road
Palatine, IL. 60067
847-755-2600

This high school located in the northwestern suburbs boasts at least three different spirits to its hallowed halls. Students are well aware of the many spooks along Cuba Road and nearby White Cemetery but are quite sure that their Alma Mater is truly haunted by some strange spectral visitors from beyond.

Noisy ghosts are said to haunt Kolze Auditorium including one that likes to play with the spring-loaded seats during dress rehearsals. Others, even faculty, have told tales of spotlights being shone on them when no spotlight operators were present. Maybe it's just trying to "grab the spotlight"?

A roaming ghost, not tied down to one particular site, has been reported throughout the school but most often in Room 122-S. Teachers have heard ghostly sighs and moans emanating from the empty room or even while some are inside finishing up their typing chores. Other sounds include rustling papers even though none are actually seen to move. In the Fall of 1999, a student described her encounter of a pneumatic machine going on by itself. She wasn't very comfortable there for much longer by herself.

The swimming pool and area is the home to the last ghost often reported by students and teachers a lot and may indeed be traceable through past history. Since the late 1970s, swim team members and others have sensed odd things probably due to a freshman student who perished while swimming laps. Swimming trunks have been seen both floating in the pool itself or laying on the locker room floor, long after the others have been picked up and put away. The violent sound of lockers being slammed resound through the empty locker room and swimmers claim that the water close to where the girl died is much colder than the surrounding water. Many actually tend to shy away from that spot.

At times, coaches and teachers, who arrive early to open up the pool area often, describe a violet haze or mist that hovers over the pool before gradually and slowly disappearing from sight.

Perhaps the spirit of that unfortunate drowning victim prefers to stay in the one area that she truly enjoyed while alive. Perhaps she is still yet trying to complete her laps throughout eternity?

South Side Haunts

Chinatown
200 Block of West 22nd Place
Chicago, IL.

The first Chinese immigrants arrived in Chicago in the 1870s, long after the other Chinese had settled in California, Oregon and Washington. It began with the completion of the transcontinental railroad which recruited Chinese as almost 80% of its workforce. During the 1950s and '60s, the Chinese population in Chicago doubled itself from 7,000 to 14,000. By 1970, Chicago ranked fourth in Chinese population in America. The first Chinese community was built around the Van Buren and Clark Streets. In 1905, due to the ill treatment of Chinese in California, there was a boycott of American trade in China.

When news came to Chicago, the presence of Chinese aroused hostile feelings and suspicion. Landlords raised the rents of houses occupied by Chinese to such a significant rate that most occupants could not afford to pay. About half the Chinese population in Chicago was forced to move south to Cermak and Wentworth Avenues, an Italian and Croatian neighborhood.

It was made possible by a series of 10-year leases on buildings that were contracted through the H.O. Stone Company by members of The On Leong Businessmen's Association. Cermak Road and Wentworth Avenue soon became the hub of Chinatown.

But after the Chinese had settled in the vicinity, some major city projects were taking place in the area. Extension of Cermak Road for the 1933 World's Fair cut the housing in half. Construction of the Dan Ryan and Stevenson Expressways in the 1950s halved its size again. Even more housing was demolished in 1969 after the state announced the construction of the Franklin Street extension to the Dan Ryan, a project that never materialized.

The present Chinatown consists of eight blocks, bounded by Cermak Road, the railway embankment, East at Wentworth and South on 26th Street. Affordable housing in the current area is limited. The two public housing projects, Archer Courts within Chinatown itself, and the Armor Square in the peripheral area are mainly occupied by African American and are avoided by most Chinese because of the racial stigma.

Later research suggests that the area on which Chinatown in now located was once an Indian burial ground. And, the one area most Chinese agree is the most haunted is the 200 block of West 22nd Place. This area has mostly homes but does contain two restaurants and the Chinatown Community Center.

According to local historians, a number of homes are allegedly haunted due to suicides by hangings and others which have caught fire and burnt to the ground mysteriously. Ghosts were thought to be the cause in both cases. Power surges and outages plague this area and Commonwealth Edison is constantly out here working on lines to restore power to the community.

The Triple Crown, located at 211 West 22nd Place, was a former apartment, now a restaurant is haunted because of a suicide on the site when it was an apartment building. A helpful ghost has been experienced here. One who pitches in when the place is extremely busy. Dirty dishes and silverware that were piled up minutes ago are often found washed and neatly stacked by the unseen. A strange figure has been reported in the washrooms, the location where the alleged suicide occurred. The figure is semi-transparent and surely not a human being!

Just slightly west of the restaurant another structure was haunted during the 1970s by poltergeist activity. The basement flat was the scene of moving objects in the kitchen and the curtains which moved by themselves. Again, supposedly a suicide by hanging occurred here a number of years ago.

The Chinatown Community Center, opened in 1963, is at the end of 22nd Place and has two large marble "foo dogs" and a giant bronze statue of Confucius in front. The women's washroom is told to be haunted by the ghost of a little old lady. Located on the second floor of the center, she disappears before she has the chance to be investigated by eye witnesses.

St. Therese School, which is located at 247 West 23rd Street, had been located in the Old Chinatown City Hall, which is not only said to be haunted, but is also located on that block where a cemetery once stood. Although the building of St. Therese School did not open until 1961, the institution itself had actually begun two decades earlier from the inspiration of then Archbishop of Chicago George Cardinal Mundelein. At that time, great efforts were being made to organize the Chinese Catholics of Chicago. Cardinal Mundelein worked closely with Nanking's Bishop Paul Yu-Pin, and they ultimately appointed Father John T.S. Mao to take on this huge endeavor.

St. Therese School opened in 1941 as a part of Father Mao's efforts, operating out of the On Leong Merchants; Association building at the corner of 22nd and Wentworth. Classes began that year under the direction of the Notre Dame Sisters, and the first diplomas were awarded in 1942. In 1945, the Maryknoll Sisters assumed responsibility for the school, and soon they began conducting a social service program, benefiting both students and parishioners. By the end of the 1950s, the school had become such a success that the rented classrooms could no longer accommodate all the children and nearly half the student body had to travel by bus to attend classes at nearby St. Paul's School.

Through the generous support of donors, a new single-school building was erected at 247 W. 23rd Street, home of the present-day school. The architectural firm of Kefer & Cronin designed the steel and glass structure in a style reminiscent of old Chinese pagodas, symbolizing and representing the Chinatown community.

At its current location, the school has a Chinese facade, which despite being less than 30-years-old, looks like it has been left to fall apart. The windows look worn and the paint is peeling. An 86-year-old woman related information about what was there before the school.

She had lived across from the school for some number of years between the 1930s and 1969 when the school was built. For many years, she said, the land that the school is on was an empty lot, while the rest of the block had been built on. In the late 1950s, a construction company built some homes, and couldn't sell them. After quite a while, the homes were sold to African-American families, who moved in and made them their homes for a few years.

By the mid-1960s, all the African-American families had moved out. The woman said it wasn't from racial problems, as they got along with everyone. They just sold and left without telling the neighbors. The houses were put up for sale and never sold. The houses then began to fall into disrepair quite quickly, and in 1969, the Archdiocese offered to buy the property if the homes were removed. The school was built, and so the haunting began.

In 1992, the school's religion coordinator, a nun, began to share this story with other nuns and teachers in the school. It had happened to her during the Christmas vacation.

She and two other nuns had been in their living area on the third floor when she left the other two sisters to get something from her bedroom. The nun's bedrooms had no doors, but rather a rod with curtain which began 14 inches from the top of the doorway and stopped about the same distance from the floor.

In her bedroom, she faced the window which was opposite the doorway, and was looking through her things to locate something. Then a female voice called her name, to which she answered, "wait." Upon hearing it again, she glanced sideways and got a peripheral view of shoes under the curtain, and again answered, "Wait." The third time her name was called; she turned completely around, and not seeing shoes, angrily opened her curtain and said, "What is it?" No one was there, so she stopped looking and returned to the living room.

She interrogated both nuns as to which one it was who called her, and after their denials and the fact that neither was wearing shoes that looked like the ones she thought she saw, she dropped the whole thing. When she later thought about it, she said she couldn't place the voice, other than it was soft-spoken and sounded like neither of the other sisters.

Another story involves two teachers.

The fifth and seventh grade teachers were the last people in the building late at night in December of 1993. The two teachers were still in their classrooms on the second floor, and poked their heads into the hall to look across at each other to ask when the other was going to leave. The two traveled home together by bus.

The seventh grade teacher was finished first and locked her room and told the other she was going to use the restroom on the first floor and to meet her at the main entrance.

Meanwhile, the fifth grade teacher, a 30-year veteran with a Master's Degree in Psychology (and is married to a doctor), was ready to leave and was locking her classroom door. While her back was to the hall (her classroom door being recessed into the wall), she glanced sideways hearing someone walk pass behind her. She immediately began calling to the person as she locked the door. She turned and walked toward the east stairwell door since that was the way the person went. She would have sworn that the figure was a woman dressed in a long white coat. She knew it wasn't the seventh grade teacher, so her walls were warning who she thought was a mother to leave the closed school.

In the stairwell, she looked up toward the third floor, and the locked floor door. She looked down toward the first and basement floor doors, and they too were locked. She walked down to the first floor and unlocked the floor door and looked around. She did the same in the basement and found no one.

When she finally met the seventh grade teacher at the front door, she asked her if the mother had gotten out ok. The seventh grade teacher didn't even know what she was talking about. No one had passed her, and the only other way out was through the east door. To do so, the mother would have had to walk through fresh snow and scale a locked fence which enclosed most of the front of the school. The snow, they saw, had no prints in it.

The third phenomenon involved the pre-school teacher who was a retired Chicago Public School special education teacher and her assistant, an older nun who lived alone in the third floor convent area, and had been a principal of a Catholic school in China years back. These stories took place between November 1995 and February 1996.

The pre-school teacher had gotten permission from the nun to use one of the unoccupied bedrooms which had a wooden door on it, to take a nap during her lunch break each day. The bedrooms were also used for storing religious books in shelves on the east wall of the room.

A friend of mine and fellow GRS member was also involved in this tale and relates the following:

"One day in late January of 1996, I was in the school's library, which was occupying what had been the nun's living room. The pre-school teacher had passed me and said hello. She entered the bedroom she had been allowed to use, and began calling my name real loud as if she was afraid of something.

"By the time I reached her, about 75 feet down the hall; she was sitting on the edge of the bed staring at the sink in the wall at the foot of the bed, still calling my name. I entered the room and asked her what was the matter, and turned to the west wall and saw the sink running water. She looked at me and said, 'I just sat down and looked out the window, and the water went on by itself. I thought Sister was crazy when she said the water was always on in this room, but it just went on with me sitting here.'

"I turned the water off, and went down to the pre-school room and asked the nun about the sink. I was concerned more about a plumbing problem. The nun looked at me and said, 'Every time I pass that room, someone has left the water on.' I think she blamed the pre-school teacher, who later claimed never to have used the old sink. 'A few times in November and December someone dumped some red stuff in the sink, and I had to clean it out every time,' the nun added wanting to get someone in trouble. No one had access to that room, nor was even authorized to be on the third floor except for the pre-school teacher, nun, janitor, principal, Chinese teacher and myself.

"I remembered seeing the pink stain myself. I had seen it a few times while looking for religious books on the bookshelves in that room before Christmas. I thought it was a rust stain from not being used over the years. The nun told me that she had scrubbed it out a few times, and almost every other day found the water running.

"The school's janitor, who is a licensed contractor by trade, checked the fittings on the sink and found nothing wrong, but replaced the washer and tightened everything just to make sure. The water still continued to go on by itself until the end of February when the problem stopped by itself.

"When the principal and I often left late, he and I went to check the basement together, as he said he felt like someone was down there watching him as he walked from one side to the other of the school hall to check the light switches and boiler controls. However, the 86-year-old woman would spend all night cooking down in the school hall prior to most fund-raisers, and never feel anything down there."

From September 1995 to April 1996, the nun often complained that the plumbing in the convent section of the third floor was developing problems. There are two restroom and shower facilities which are right next to each other. Both have four shower stalls, three toilets and three sinks. The sinks in both rooms were unaffected even though both the water supplies and sewer pipes were all connected to the toilets and showers.

The first complaint the nun had came in September 1995 when all three toilets in one facility were stopped up. The school janitor used acid to get them to go down and said since there was a second facility; the nun should stop using the bad one and only use the other one. This didn't include the shower stalls which she continued to use and the sinks.

Her next complaint was near Thanksgiving, and it was that the one shower stall in the first facility as well as a toilet was very sluggish, and she was stopping the use of the first facility all together. By January, she let them know that one toilet and two shower stalls wouldn't go down. The janitor got them down and then marked them out of order. By April, all three toilets in both facilities (total of six) wouldn't go down properly. All but one of eight showers (4 in each) wouldn't go down and the hot and cold water didn't work.

At this point, the janitor began an entire day of working on the two facilities. First, he traced all the pipes in the walls to the basement. He found that all the drain pipes went together and had no explanation why the sinks were going down and the other things weren't. But as in all buildings, he said, it could be different lines he didn't see turns in. The hot and cold worked in all the sinks, but not in the showers. Also, the toilet water was fine.

Second, he spent a couple of hours removing all the fittings from the showers. He couldn't find anything wrong with anything. He used pipe cleaners and found nothing in the pipes. Then he worked on one shower stall, and after an hour, the hot water worked fine in that one and the other ones he hadn't touched. When he worked on the cold water, the one stall shot him with a stream of cold water that soaked him. Soon all had working cold water, and again he only worked on one stall, but all began working fine.

He went into the nun's laundry room to dry his clothes in the dryer, and after 30 minutes, found out the heating element wasn't working and had to put his soaking wet clothes back on. That night, the nun used the dryer and it worked fine.

In March 1996, the school hired a 60-year-old professor from China who came on as a part-time Chinese teacher. They had him use the east corner of the library on the third floor as his office. From the day he came in, the nun began to complain someone was using her chop sticks, dishes, and then leaving them and her sink dirty. She blamed the poor Chinese teacher who claimed he never touched her kitchen and had left to each lunch at Gourmet Food's Inc., a local restaurant a block away. This continued on and off until the end of the school year in June when he and she had a big fight in the east stairwell and he thought she was crazy. She certainly acted out of character, as some heard her screaming out loud.

The school has an elevator which operates between the first and third floors, which has a 500 pound weight limit and is under strict contract by a major elevator service company. It is service monthly, along with two major servicings per year; one for the beginning of school and the second for the City of Chicago inspection.

Yet from July 1994 to June 1995, in addition to the regular service calls, nine additional paid service calls were made and three non-paid service returns. Five times the cam chain and return broke. Twice the chain was repaired and then three new chains were put in. On two occasions, the regular service man had just checked it on its monthly service. Two days later, the chain would break and he'd have to come back. He stated he serviced elevators for downtown office buildings, as well as three other elevators of identical model as the one in the school, and none of them required as much maintenance.

The nun had been stuck in it an unaccountable number of times over the years, both going up and down.

Clearly the Chinatown area has much to offer in the way of ghosts and the unexplained.

http://www.chicago-chinatown.com/

Ethyl's Party
2600 S. Wentworth Ave.
Chicago, Illinois 60616
773-276-0961

Tito's on the original edge of Chinatown was at one time a funeral home, Coletta's around 1908 which served the Italians in the area of Chinatown. The funeral director lived in the upstairs apartments. As the neighborhood changed in the 1960s and '70s, the Italians moved elsewhere and "Tito's On The Edge" came into being. It was so named because it is located on the edge of Chinatown. The restaurant operated by brothers opened up in 1995 and the regulars are local Italians and Chinese. However, one thing is certain; the place is truly haunted by those who frequent the place.

The name was most recently changed to Ethyl's Party due to a most unusual event. According to locals, there was a homeless person that had lost his wife many years ago. While attempting to cross the street one evening, he was struck and injured by a car. He was never quite the same anymore and would often wander the area screaming out his deceased wife's name, "Ethyl! Ethyl!" over and over again.

Owner Bobby Tito, always felt uncomfortable about the place. I guess part of that could be its former incarnation as a funeral home. That would surely give the creeps to most. The back room was the embalming room and downstairs is where bodies awaited, in cold storage, to be properly prepared for wakes.

Television sets display a mind of their own by constantly changing channels. The set is not defective in any way because it's happened to both the televisions in the bar area.

Apparitions have been reported including one by co-owner Russ Tito in the summer of 1995. While sleeping one night in the bar after working a number of overtime hours, he awoke and observed a figure dressed in a trench coat walk from the bar to the side door of the establishment. Described as an older man, not hazy or filmy but perfectly solid, the phantom disappeared near the stage. This area was used for wakes when it was a funeral home.

A bartender had her own sighting late at night just after the bar was closed for the evening. She was sitting with a friend reading when a huge cloud of smoke, white in color, drifted from one end of the bar to the other. Her sighting was different from the owners as this cloudy mist didn't have a recognizable form to it. However, it disappeared in the same area as the owner's ghost report. Occasionally shadowy figures are seen by patrons in the hallway and vanish quite rapidly.

Perhaps these ghosts have something to do with the building while it was being used as a funeral parlor? Or, are they still visiting their spectral deceased even though the wake area no longer exists? No one knows for sure.

Hadley Cemetery
167th and Meader Road
Will County Forest Preserves

Messenger Woods is one of Will County's oldest and most unique forest preserves. Here, visitors can enjoy one of the few remaining forests in northeastern Illinois that have not been altered by grazing, cutting, farming or development.

Considered a high-quality, old-grove forest, Messenger Woods has oak uplands and rich maple bottom lands on a rolling glacial hill terrain. Spring Creek, which runs through the preserve, has but several steep ravines. Visitors can hike or ski along two miles of looped trails that meander through this scenic preserve.

Messenger Woods is known throughout the region for its abundance of Spring wild flowers that carpet the forest floor. Watch the numerous nature photographers preach over their camera to capture the blue-eyed Mary, large-flowered trillium, wild geranium and hepatica in bloom. The biggest attraction is the Virginia bluebells, far more appear at Messenger Woods over a few fleeting weeks in April and May than anywhere else in Will County. The rare Cooper's hawk and state-endangered red-shouldered hawk nest annually in the preserve.

However, on the sinister side there have been reports of Satanism and Witchcraft (though the two are quite widely different) in the area for many years. There is also an unsubstantiated report that a young girl accidentally drove her car off a high cliff and that she now haunts the area. Other stories include murders that have occurred in the woods themselves where the unfortunate victims were found hanging from trees by police and forest rangers.

The small cemetery itself is not easy to find and is a bit off the road. While trying to research additional information regarding the cemetery, local officials that I had contacted through websites knew nothing about the graveyard and, in fact, weren't even aware that such a place even existed. Believe me, this is not a page from the Twilight Zone because I've been there personally myself on several occasions.

What initially sparked my interest were the "alleged murders" and reports that an old gravestone existed on the far side of the cemetery which supposedly contained the remains of an actual witch who was killed and buried in the cemetery. The grave was allegedly not part of the consecrated ground and soon after she was buried, townsfolk planted briars and thorn bushes on and near her grave, "to keep her soul in the ground."

I was able to find this alleged witches grave however the names and dates are so badly worn, it's almost impossible to make anything out. Was that the grave of an actual witch killed in the middle of the last century?

Then came the reports of strange balls of light that would float and waft through the cemetery at night. When police would be called to investigate, they would never find any trespassers around who might have been the source of these ghost lights.

Joliet Catholic High School
1200 N. Larkin Avenue
Joliet, IL. 60435

In the early hours of darkness, lights are turned off and locked doors slam in the old Joliet Catholic High School building on "The Hill".

And the ghost of a young priest who died in a fiery accident 29 years ago apparently continues to walk the empty hallways.

"But now that we know he was a priest - that he is a good ghost - we feel safe that he is looking out for us," said a former custodian, who works the midnight shift in the school. "He is looking out for us especially after realizing what we went through with the tornado."

The custodian, who was 49 at the time of the interview, didn't want her name used, and was a 14-year-veteran, at that time, of the Plainfield School District. She said she was a little frightened when she first heard about the ghost.

She heard the tale from construction workers who were remodeling the building, just before Plainfield High School moved into its new quarters.

"I really don't believe in ghosts, but it was kind of scary in the beginning," she said. "But I feel much better in knowing that he was a priest. Now I find myself talking to him as I work."

She said that as she runs a vacuum cleaner, she says things like, "Oh, pardon me, Father, but I have to make this noise while I clean."

"Then I think to myself, 'you're nuts,'" she said.

But, she said for one week a light to the outside that she kept turning on was turned off by someone. She accused another custodian of trying to scare her because it kept happening. He denied doing it.

Then one night while she was cleaning on the first floor, a door slammed on the second floor. But all of those doors were locked. Other locked doors have slammed since then, she said.

She said another custodian working on the third floor saw a shadow and heard footsteps one night.

"But I'm not afraid now," she said. "I know if he's there, he is a good spirit who is looking out for us."

The ghost, according to local tradition, is said to be the Rev. Kellen Ryan, who taught at Catholic High from 1966 until his death in 1972.

On Saturday, March 5, 1972, he drove into Chicago to visit his parents. Early that Sunday morning he headed home for Joliet. But he fell asleep at the wheel of his car.

The time was about 4:10 a.m. when his car left McCarthy Road near Lemont and hit a garage, a tree and a telephone pole. The car erupted into flames and killed the 33-year-old priest.

The legend of Kellen Ryan's ghost was born the same day he died. Another priest who had been a close friend heard the jukebox in the cafeteria go on real loud that evening. But when he checked, the jukebox was playing with no record on the turntable. He immediately thought of Father Ryan, who had often turned the jukebox down when he was in the cafeteria.

Exactly one month after his death, the dean who replaced him reported seeing a ghost in his bedroom. The ghost was dressed in a Carmelite habit and was sitting in a rocking chair.

Another priest reported seeing the ghost at the foot of his bed. That priest said the ghost left him with a feeling of happiness rather than fright.

The legacy of the ghost continued to grow. There were several more sightings.

For example, a janitor cleaning the third floor one evening saw a priest walking toward him. The figure was wearing a habit with the hood pulled up. The janitor even spoke a greeting as the figure walked past him.

The janitor turned and looked at the figure, which had turned and was looking at him. The janitor said there was no face visible inside the hood.

Some say the lights in Father Ryan's former classroom, Room 306, occasionally go on in the middle of the night. As the tales of the ghost were told and retold, they were probably embellished along the way.

But seniors used to be invited to spend the night in the locked school on the anniversary of Father Ryan's death. As many as 100 boys would spend the night telling the ghost tales while playing sports in the gymnasium.

One anniversary night, the burglar alarm went off in a room on the other side of the building. This was the same room that Father Ryan had used for an office. Perhaps the ghost was telling the boys he remained with them in spirit.

And maybe, just maybe, he's still there looking over the new coed student body this time. But don't worry folks; he is definitely a friendly ghost!

Justice Public Library
7641 Oak Grove Avenue
Justice, IL. 60458
708-496-1790

Beth Mueller and Arlene Ramey Robison started this library from a small, abandoned yellow house on the corner of 76th and Oak Grove Avenue in September of 1978. They were to operate a trial library here for the village for a one-year period. However, after the year was up, if the library was a failure, it would have been closed up for good. Due to generous donations from the village, for the empty building, federal grants and a great supply of books and other materials from a failed demo library, Flagg Creek, it began to slowly take shape.

The first director was Gail Langer and the push was on to get the word out to local residents of their new library. However, the needs of the community were greater than expected and in 1995, a newer and larger public library was built directly across the street from the original facility.

The first library was rumored to have been haunted mostly by poltergeist-type activity, i.e. movements of objects, mostly books. When the new library was built, it seems that the ghost packed up and headed for its larger headquarters.

Within five years in April and May of 2000, books have been picked up and neatly stacked near the ends of the bookshelves. The subject matter of the displaced books was often about cats, biographies and historical events. Most believe the ghost to be that of a former staff member.

A very interesting sighting took place by an outsider. A motorist who simply pulled into the parking lot of the library late one evening to make an emergency call on his cell phone. He happened to glance into the library and observed a shadowy figure pulling library books off the shelves and dumping them unto the floor! No staff or librarian was present at that time of the night!

Jane McGuire of the library guesses that the ghost could possibly be one Helen Hyry, a former board of director's member. Hyry's comments of never having a male director of the library while she was on the board might be the reason of the phenomena since the former director was indeed a male. When he moved to Canada to accept another position there, the phenomena seems to have died down quite a bit. It's actually quite quiet and peaceful there, as libraries go.

http://www.justicepubliclibrary.com/

Maple Tree Inn
13301 S. Old Western Avenue
Blue Island, IL. 60406
708-388-3461

Often, the Halloween season is a time of year when people let their imaginations get the better of them.

Because of the occasion they may be more hesitant to go down into a dark basement and are more likely to believe they hear strange noises coming from the attic.

Those so afflicted should take heed if they plan to visit the Maple Tree Inn restaurant in Blue Island. The entire establishment has been turned into a haunted restaurant that manufactures an abundance of ghoulish effects.

Actually, according to owner Charlie Orr, the restaurant has been thought to be haunted for years.

"There have been some weird things happening around here ever since I bought the place 10 years ago," he said.

Orr says he believes some of the weirdness could be traced back to the building's original owner, the late Helen Sadunas. Sadunas ran the restaurant; Helen's Olde Lantern, in that location for years and lived above her business.

"I don't think she was very happy that I ended up with this place because I changed the original name. She was in business for close to 50 years here and always wanted to have her name associated with it," Orr said.

"When she first put it up for sale she would not sell it to me for that reason, so she sold it to Tony and John Molinaro."

When Orr, who was running the Maple Tree Inn farther north on Western Avenue, heard later that the Molinaros were selling the old building, he made sure he was the new owner.

"After I bought the place from those guys, I kept the name Maple Tree Inn," he said.

Now, when strange things take place in the restaurant, many believe it may be the work of Sadunas.

"It's never been anything too nasty," said the restaurant's chef, Tom Hecht. "But about two years ago, I felt someone tap me on the shoulder when I was in the basement. The problem was, nobody else was there.

"There have been other times, too, when there's been a weird feeling like there's a strange presence in the room that you're not seeing."

Perhaps tempting fate, Orr is celebrating Halloween by having his restaurant turned into a haunted house that spares no detail. The decorating was done by Marybeth Brown, an interior designer who specializes in haunted houses. She immediately saw the potential in the Blue Island building.

"Marybeth visited the restaurant one time and told me that it would make a great haunted house," Orr recalled.

Brown, a Michigan resident, recalled liking what she saw at the Maple Tree Inn.

"I liked the fact that it was an old Victorian-style house. It just looked the part, even from the outside," she said.

Her decorations were elaborate enough that it took close to a week to finish the work.

"I work fast, but it still took about six days to complete that job," she said.

What she put together was five rooms with a different haunted scene in each. She also piped horror-type music into the rooms, including one of the bathrooms, which has the theme from "Psycho" playing.

Skeletons, witches, coffins and vampires abound throughout the restaurant. Along with these, are some more unique items such as pictures with eyes that move and a Ouija board that seems to move on its own.

"I'm not really into blood and guts as much as just creating an eerie scene for people to be taking in," Brown said.

A collector of all things scary, she has been designing haunted homes for 15 years.

"It began when I decorated my own house in the Lakeview neighborhood in Chicago," Brown said. "It started out being just for trick-or-treaters, but eventually, the crowds grew so large that there was an hour wait to tour the house. I've been doing this kind of thing ever since I was a kid and I designed everyone's costumes at Halloween."

These days Brown is getting into the act herself by dressing up as "Death" and lying in one of the coffins at the Maple Tree Inn.

"I'm hoping the customers get some fun out of this. I'm really not trying to scare anyone too much," she said.

This is especially true for children who Brown does not allow to get too frightened.

"When I used to do this act at the haunted houses, I would actually get up out of the coffin and ask the parents to take their kids out if they seemed too scared," she said.

As for the Maple Tree Inn, the restaurant's veranda includes a stage area that is designed to resemble a graveyard. The Graveyard Blues Band has been playing there every Saturday night in October and also performed on Halloween, of course.

"I've always been fascinated by cemeteries," Brown said. "I actually own a lot of real tombstones, but the ones I used here are made of Styrofoam."

Brown said she has heard the stories about Sadunas haunting the place, but didn't encounter anything while doing the decorating late at night at the Maple Tree Inn.

"I get so involved in my work, that I wasn't giving it a second thought, even though I was alone in the place," she said.

Despite this, Brown does not dismiss the possibility that the rumors about Sadunas haunting the place could be true.

"I definitely believe in that kind of thing," she said.

Mt. Auburn Cemetery
4101 S. Oak Park Avenue
Stickney, IL. 60402
708-749-0022

In 1895, Mt. Auburn was founded. It consisted of over 100 acres and was designed and laid out under the personal supervision of Mr. O.C. Simonds, renowned landscape architect.

It was the first cemetery in the Chicago area to be developed with park lawn type sections using only flush markers, which resulted in beautiful garden-like sections. This was revolutionary at the time, and as time passed this concept was embraced throughout the nation.

Some of this information was reproduced from the 87th General Assembly Senate Resolution No. 51 on display in the cemetery office, which Mt. Auburn received February 13, 1991 in recognition of its environmental and other contributions to the community.

The entrance gate and office building, dating back to 1895, once served as the Village of Stickney Village Hall until 1919, after which the village arranged other facilities. There is a Woodlawn Veteran's Section dedicated in 1938. This became the first of two veteran sections when the Elmwood Veterans Section was developed. Of particular interest to veterans was the announcement of a special program to provide free burial space for veterans. This program is still available to honorably discharged vets today.

On the far south end of the cemetery is a Chinese Pagoda where, every summer, survivors of the deceased burn ghost money for the dead at the pagoda, so the dead will have money in the next world. This is a common Chinese believe as they are heavily into ancestral world. The site of the pagoda is located in a large, predominately Chinese section of the cemetery.

In the Garden of Devotion section of Mt. Auburn rests a large Carrara marble sculpture, quarried and sculpted in Carrara, some sixty miles northeast of Florence, Italy. It's fashioned in the shape of a large open bible and depicts the Lord's Prayer on one side and the 23rd Psalm on the opposite side. It's at or near this large white monument, nicknamed "The Book Monument", by local residents is where a phantom female has been seen throughout the years.

An anonymous friend of mine who works at a local library did some in depth research and inquiries about the alleged ghost stories.

"I anonymously called the Stickney-Forest View Library to see if they had any information about Mt. Auburn. I talked to Peggy (pseudonym) and she told me that they had only current ghost books and directories, no old ones. She offered to call Mt. Auburn to ask them directly about their hauntings. I told her they would hang up on her. She also offered to ask some members of the Golden Agers Club, and said she would do additional research on it from other town and township publications. She became really involved with the idea and said she would be really interested in such information herself.

"When I called her back, I got an entirely different attitude. First, she told me that she had called the cemetery, and they said they have no ghosts. Second, she told me she talked to a couple life-long residents who claimed they heard no such stories. She never mentioned the Golden Agers. The rest of the conversation and her overall attitude were evasive. Then she kept saying that on one in the town ever saw anything, and wanted to get me off the phone as soon as possible.

"Apparently, she talked to someone at the cemetery who had her reprimanded for even asking. Several years ago, the Stickney-Forest View Library was going to have a ghost-related presentation, I don't know by whom, but rumor had it that once it was advertised in the Life Newspaper, Mt. Auburn had said something to have it stopped. It was scheduled and even noted in the newspapers, then I found out it was canceled after many people had gone to Stickney to sign up for it.

"My mother had talked to a few women back in the late 1970s and early 1980s that lived across from the cemetery. The one woman who lived south of the Jehovah Witnesses Kingdom Hall across from the cemetery's entrance had said she and her husband were afraid to go out their front door after dark because of what they would see if they looked into the cemetery. In fact, this woman had been offered an evening job phone soliciting by the cemetery, but said she didn't want to cross the street and walk (the 250 feet) into the cemetery after dark.

"These women were in their later 60s or early 70s and said they didn't like to look out their windows after dark. 'There is a lot going on that can't be explained,' they said.

"When my sister and I attended St. Pius X School, which is right across from Mt. Auburn at 43rd Street, we heard two major stories over the years. The first was that a ghostly woman floated through the cemetery at night. The second was that a ghostly house also moved through the cemetery. The one thing also mentioned was that the house floated quite a few feet above the ground as it moved. We had heard these from adults as well as other kids. These stories were told and retold over a nine-year period.

"Prompted by stories we heard in school, friends of our family, a 35-year-old woman and her 65-year-old father walked past on Halloween night in 1983. They had lived in Stickney for twenty-five-years, they said, and they had never heard the story before. When visiting the cemetery that night, they claimed they saw the figure of a woman in a white gown standing near the "Book Monument". They added they felt the figure saw or felt them and then faded away.

"One personal note: our one and a half-year-old and thirteen-year-old Labrador Retrievers both acted strange and would stare into the northeast section of the cemetery behind the stone picture of Jesus Christ and across from it by the east fence."

After the inquiries were made by my anonymous friend, he noted:

"Mt. Auburn Cemetery has had the light turned off which was shining on the Book Monument since early September (1998). I have heard from a Cicero Auxiliary Officer that the Stickney Police have been getting calls for about two months from people passing, neighbors across the street and the cemetery office itself to double patrols through the cemetery because of reports of people roaming through the cemetery, moving lights (that look like candles), a woman who walks around the one lighted outdoor mausoleum in a white robe, what looks like people hooded in black gowns and red lights of moving and parked cars among the monuments. Of the many calls, and the cemetery's plea for additional patrols, the Stickney Police only ejected a car of teens once and has found nothing when responding to reports."

According to another source who wishes to remain anonymous, even the nuns who taught in St. Pius knew about the ghost stories from the time the school opened in the mid-1950s. In June 1977, the Sisters of St. Casimir quit the school abruptly for no reasons and many people said they were afraid of the ghosts across the street. Many of the nuns left the convent to become regular people and get married during the 1950s and although the school had been closed since 1966, they still leave nuns to live in the convent of the abandoned school. One of the former principals and two other nuns at the time knew the ghost stories very well and were afraid of living in the convent above the south-wing of the school.

The nuns from the Sisters of St. Casimir had to be scared of the ghosts across the street because so many of the nuns left the school after a short time. Between 1954 and 1968 St. Pius had 11 nun principals because none of them wanted to stay. A former principal who served from 1968 to 1977 often told parents she saw several unexplained things from driving on Oak Park Avenue at night. She also had constant trouble starting her car and the mechanics could never find the reason. She would often sit in the driver's seat and say a prayer and try again to start it, and often it would start.

The nuns also knew about the sexual pervert who went running through the cemetery with and without his clothes during the 1970s even attacking people by the Stickney-Forest View Library after dark. Those stories were published in The Life newspaper back in the 1970s many times.

A former pastor used to stand in front of the Rectory saying he was watching the gnomes running around playing tag around the monuments. He was the only one who would voice his opinion on ghosts, and soon taken out of the parish and retired somewhere. And yet another former pastor went into his car that was parked on Oak Park Avenue in front of the Rectory and died of a heart attack while looking at a ghostly apparition in the cemetery.

The most haunted places of the cemetery are the areas that can be seen from the fence on Oak Park Avenue and across the whole south side of the cemetery behind the homes that go from East or Oak Park Avenues on 41st Street. The people who live in the homes to the north of the cemetery are always selling to move away.

There are other tales of both red and white lights being seen in the cemetery after dark and strange clouds and cars but the police have never been able to find anything.

The cemetery eventually relit the monument with a much dimmer illumination in February of 1999. Or, well after the Halloween frenzy had died down.

Frank Nitti's Suicide Location
Near Toys 'R Us, Illinois Central Railroad Tracks
Cermak Road just west of Harlem Avenue
North Riverside, IL. 60546

Francesco Raffaele Nitto, better known as, Frank "The Enforcer" Nitti has been portrayed by Hollywood as a viscous gangland thug, Capone trigger man and smooth talking cocky gangster. In Brian De Palmer's 1987 movie "The Untouchables", the cinema going and video-watching public were introduced to Nitti as the nemesis of Elliot Ness and his band of federal agents. The movie even goes as far to show Nitti dying at the hands of Ness, falling from the roof of the Chicago court house where Capone was being tried which is completely untrue. He eventually died by his own hands.

Frank Nitti began his criminal career as a barber with a rather shady clientele. His customers would come to him to fence various items of stolen merchandise. It was while in this role that he came to the attention of John Torrio and Al Capone since he had a proven network of underworld characters able to peddle illegal booze. Nitti became a whiz at smuggling Canadian whiskey into Chicago and to the various distribution ports throughout the city.

By the mid-twenties, he was a high-ranking member of the Capone Mob. With the conviction of Al Capone in 1929, Nitti became the boss of the Chicago Mob. At least that is what the press and law enforcement agencies believed. So high profile was the coverage of the mob in those days, that Nitti was a natural choice for the press. Nitti probably believed it himself. In fact, it was Paul "The Waiter" Ricca who carried the flame of the

Mob after Capone. Ricca was quite happy to let Nitti think he had control, but there were often times when Ricca would countermand a Nitti decision with a quick, "We'll do it this way - and let's say no more about it."

Nitti was never made a member of the Commission (a board of directors of all the Mafioso families) but Ricca was, secretly, without Nitti's knowledge. It was only the presses spotlight on Nitti that made him important. This would draw attention away from the real workings of the Chicago Outfit. On December 19, 1932, Nitti had a run in with the O'Banion/Moran crew, now run by Ted Newberry. Newberry had the Mayor of Chicago, Anton Cermak, on his payroll and used his influence to have police sent to one of Nitti's hangouts at 221 N. LaSalle, to have him arrested.

A gunfight erupted and Nitti was badly wounded. He lingered at deaths door for a time but eventually recovered only to face trial for allegedly shooting Police Sergeant Lang during the gunfight engineered by Newberry. Mayor Cermak put Nitti on trial for the shooting of Lang but the jury at the trial became convinced that Lang had shot himself in order to look like a hero. The trial ended in a hung jury, Nitti walked and Lang got fired from the force.

During the trial Cermak was shot by a fanatic, Guiseppe Zangara, in Miami, Florida on February 15, 1933 when he went to congratulate President-elect Franklin D. Roosevelt. As the shots rang out, a nearby photographer joked, "Just like Chicago, eh mayor?" Cermak had been hit in the lung and later died of his wound. Before he died, he is reported to have said to the President, "I am glad it was me instead of you."

Newberry was taken out about three weeks after the Lang and Nitti shootout. Newberry was blown away with shotguns and .45s on Lake Shore Drive and his body was buried in a ditch in Porter County, Indiana. The Outfit continued to carry on business as usual with the Nitti/Ricca leadership into the 1940s. It was on November 29, 1940, that Nitti was indicted with other mob figures for influencing the Chicago Bartenders and Beverage Dispensers Union of the AFL (Local 278). Nitti was accused of installing mob members in positions of power in the union and forcing the sale of beverages from mob-run breweries. The whole trial rested on the testimony of one man, George McLane. McLane was the president of this union and he followed the orders from Nitti and others under pain of death. The pressure eventually got to McLane and he went to the authorities. However, before McLane could repeat his allegations under oath in court, the Mob had a quiet word with him. He was promised that if he went through with his testimony, his wife would be mailed to him in small pieces, bit by bit.

The day came and McLane was called to testify. His answer to every question was, "I must refuse to answer on the grounds that to do so might incriminate me." The case was dropped.

Nitti got into trouble again in 1943 when he was indicted for extorting the major movie studios in Hollywood in what came to be called the Hollywood Extortion Case. Nitti masterminded a plot with several other mobsters where they gained control of the

International Alliance of Theatrical Stage Employees (IATSE). Then, the heat was turned on the Hollywood movie studios. If they didn't pay up, their stage hands and other workers could be used against them to ruin them. Warner Brothers paid, RKO paid, MGM and Fox paid. Everyone was paying up and the whole set-up looked set to be a big money earner for the mob. That was until a Chicago news reporter began asking questions when he saw Willie Bioff, one of the mobs men in the union, at a big Hollywood party. The reporter was Westbrook Pegler, a nationally syndicated reporter. He recognized Bioff as a one time pimp from Chicago and wondered why he was moving in such high society circles. When he found out what a big man Bioff had become, he began to look into it.

It was soon discovered that Bioff still owed Illinois State for a conviction for pandering. He was arrested and jailed for six months. After his release, he was indicted again along with the other mob man in IATSE, George E. Browne, for the extortion of the movie theaters. They had to appear before a Federal Grand Jury in New York and were questioned about their association with the Mob. Bioff and Browne were both found guilty but rather than do hard time, they decided to rat on their Mob controllers.

As a result, indictments were brought against Frank Nitti, Paul Ricca and others. They were called to stand trial later that year in New York. A meeting was called at Frank Nitti's house in Riverside, Illinois after the arraignment and Nitti was attacked by the other indicted members of the case about his bad handling of the whole affair. Bioff and Browne should have never have been allowed to testify. He was told by Paul Ricca to be a 'stand-up-guy' and take the rap for all of them since Bioff and Browne were his guys and so his responsibility. Nitti disagreed with Ricca and argued back that they all shared the responsibility for the whole fiasco and then ordered them all to leave. Essentially, Nitti had now broken the Mafia code of honor by not taking the heat for his failures. Nitti had previously done 18 months in jail on an income tax evasion charge and did not want to spend another day in a 9 by 6 cell. He was acutely claustrophobic and the thought made him unstable including that of losing his control of the mob.

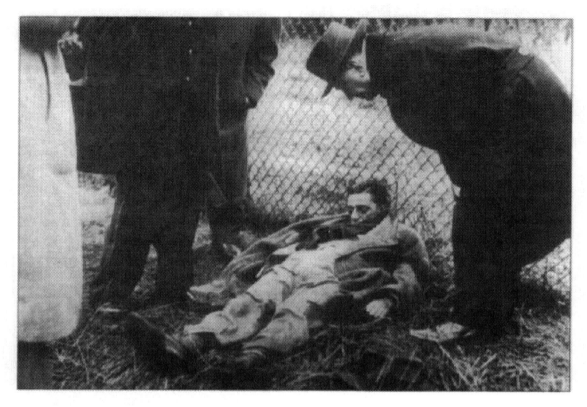

The day after the argument with Ricca, on March 19, 1943, Nitti went for a walk along the Illinois Central Railroad tracks near his home, 712 Selbourne Road in Riverside, across from the Municipal Tuberculosis Sanitarium, and blew his brains out with a pistol. The resulting trial in New York found all the defendants guilty and sentenced them all to ten years in prison.

According to eyewitness accounts, Nitti missed his temple with the first shot but then calmly tried again and succeeded. He was later laid to rest in suburban Mount Carmel Cemetery in Hillside, Illinois within steps of his former boss, Al Capone. The inscription on his tombstone read, "There is no life except by death." The location is marked today by an Olive Garden Restaurant, Toys 'R Us and a huge shopping mall. The railroad tracks are still there and aren't used that often.

Strong feelings can be encountered at the site where Nitti committed suicide. Others have seen a ghostly figure pacing the area when the tragedy took place many years ago. In September 1993, a local who works very close to the site reported seeing a shadowy figure walking somewhat westbound along the tracks. Towards, what we would assume to be his final destination, Mt. Carmel Cemetery!

Werewolf Run
Sacred Heart Cemetery
101st & Kean Avenue
Palos Hills, IL. 60465

A small little-known cemetery right on the edge of the Cook County Forest Preserve district has been the site of local legends and alleged phantom animals for years. One urban legend tells of a tragic car crash in the 1950s in which the husband and wife were killed on the spot; however the baby was thrown from the vehicle and somehow survived. The child was never found, but instead of dying from the cold, the elements and lack of food, apparently thrived and, according to the legend, was raised by the wildlife.

The baby grew a thick coat of gray hair and lived just on the very edge of the encroaching civilization. Motorists would occasionally catch a glimpse of this creature in their headlights as they traveled through the area in the evening. However, history tells us that no such accident ever occurred there but the stories persist.

In the late 1970s a suburban housewife had a frightening encounter when a manlike creature bounded out of the neighboring woods directly into the path of her truck. She nearly hit the creature dead-on but instead it only glanced off the mirror, ripping it from its hinges. She thought about stopping incase she had hit an animal like a deer but decided against it due to the late hour and lack of physical evidence of a possible fatality.

A local avid horseback rider experienced something that still gives her the goose bumps even today. She was riding in the vicinity of Sacred Heart Cemetery in the summer of 1986 during a weekday, so the trails were virtually empty at the time. She decided to go down a smaller trail that is rarely used until her regular mare began to get highly agitated over something. She decided to take the animal back to the stables where it took quite a time in quieting down the horse.

Another rider had a similar experience in almost the exact same area when they heard a horrible commotion in some nearby bushes. It was as though someone or something was violently shaking the bush with an extreme amount of force. Suddenly as they approached the suspect bushes, the movement abruptly stopped. A thorough search of the bushes and immediate area revealed nothing that could have caused this incident.

Allegedly a weathered, worn gravestone in a far corner of the cemetery marked the location where "werewolf?" was buried. In the late 1970s a section of the cemetery fence, which is simple cyclone fencing, was pulled down and bent up with what locals described as "superhuman strength". The werewolf gravestone supposedly disappeared a number of years ago and since then; there haven't been anymore werewolf sightings.

However, passing motorists still describe seeing phantom animals that appear and disappear in the high-beams as they travel along Kean Avenue. These animals could be real wild animals except that they suddenly appear in the middle of the road rather than running from one side or another and disappear with moving to the left or right of approaching vehicles.

West Side Haunts

Al Capone's Hideaway and Speakeasy
35W337 Riverside Drive
St. Charles, IL. 60174
847-741-1244

Gladys Meyers still winds her way down to Al Capone's Hideaway for a few beers and some good conversation in the big house that sits on the shore of the Fox River, just 40 miles west of Chicago.

It's not hard for her to find the place as it is for the newcomers to the restaurant and speakeasy in the northwest suburban Valley View (between St. Charles and Elgin on the Fox River). The beer probably doesn't taste the same to her as it does to newcomers either.

That's because back in 1927 (until 1938), when she was Gladys Reitmayer, she and her husband owned the reputed Al Capone hideout. Until "Scarface" took over, they made their own beer in a hidden cellar behind the chicken coop and pumped it to their thirsty

Prohibition Era patrons through an intricate copper tubing system that remains underground to this day.

Bill Brooks, Al Capone's present owner, says the 77-year-old Elgin resident hasn't lost her spunk that carried her through the police raids, barroom brawls and three marriages and divorces to the man who built Reitmayer's Beer Garden in 1917.

Chicago boosted many bootlegging syndicates at the time, according to Mrs. Meyers, and rival gang members from a few would visit Reitmayer's every other month, each suspecting the other was selling beer to the couple.

"They were always takin' samples," recalls Mrs. Meyers. "Snoopers, we call 'em. The State's Attorney wished us good luck," Mrs. Meyer chuckled. "He was a good friend of ours after we paid all the fines and he got my divorces."

The Brooks have done a great job of recapturing the atmosphere of the Prohibition days in their speakeasy. All patrons enter by way of the stairway where the famous beer cooler (that held 500 to 600 fifths of beer) once stood. They purchased the establishment in December of 1973.

Ghosts are present in the old building. Annamae Mosher, Claudia Brook's mother noticed that a swinging door between the bar and the dining room would often swing open by itself as though someone was going to and fro.

The second floor also appears to harbor some ghosts as poltergeist-type occurrences have been witnessed by some. The place settings on one particular table would always be in a state of disarray. Napkins are often found on the floor near the suspect table. Perhaps we just have a ghost whose table manners aren't the greatest? Surely a place worth visiting for the history and the fine food!

http://www.al-capone.com/steakhouse/

Allstate Arena
6920 N. Mannheim Road
Rosemont, IL. 60018
847-635-6601

Newly renovated in 1999, the Allstate Arena (formerly The Rosemont Horizon, built in 1979), is one of the crown jewels in the village of Rosemont, Illinois. The $20 million renovation made the Allstate Arena a state-of-the-art facility. The Arena hosts over 150 events annually, attracting an average of 1.5 million audience members to witness some of the world's top musical performer, exciting sports events and fun-for-everyone family entertainment. It is the home for the DePaul Blue Demons basketball team, the Chicago Wolves hockey team and many other events. It is also apparently haunted.

During construction of the then Rosemont Horizon, the roof caved in and killed several construction workers. There is little talk about the ghosts and the owners pooh-

pooh the idea of any spectral activity.

There are constant reports of hammering sounds within the building especially during the wee early morning hours, even though there is no one around and no construction being performed. It's thought by some to be those three workers who fell to their deaths when the roof collapsed. The additional sounds of footsteps and dragging chains, right out of A Christmas Carol, is sometimes heard in an underground walkway that connects the former Rosemont to the Skyline Room.

Many security personnel often complain of being followed by spectral footfalls, only to turn around and find no one following them down the darkened corridors. Others will not even walk their beat at night without another security officer for comfort and companionship. Perhaps this will go on for quite a time and security is reluctant to discuss their encounters publicly.

http://www.allstatearena.com/

Alonzi's Villa (former)
8828 Brookfield Road
Brookfield, IL. 60513
708-485-5443

Alonzi's Villa is a nice place to eat but at one time a good place to bowl. Formerly a bowling alley, built in 1936, it then became the restaurant Chalet. However, when Mike and Pat Alonzi purchased the building in the fall of 1989, they renamed it Alonzi's Villa. Right away their daughter, Trisha, would often hear voices upstairs in the storage room. Voices that were unfamiliar but friendly and would often just say, "Hello, there." The voice was that of a little girl and Trisha was a bit startled and frightened by a voice with no body.

The Alonzi's pet, Duchess, a German Shepard would be heard upstairs running around and, it seemed to the Alonzis, playing with someone or something. Other sounds include that of another dog growling, one that was surely not Duchess. And, name calling of various staff members including Pat became a common occurrence in the restaurant. It always happens just before they open the place for business when only the staff is present but no customers. Strange footsteps are also heard pacing back and forth upstairs when no one is present.

Pat has seen strange shadowy figures on the walls and sometimes just walks swiftly by her. She wasn't scared of these visitors but would invite them to watch her go about her daily business.

Rick "Elvis" Saucedo, a well-known local Elvis impersonator, has been there a number of times for performances. He has experienced unearthly coldness and warmness on the second floor. He believed the place to be haunted as well. He even brought some offerings for the ghost including a doll and a holy candle, as he thought the ghost might be that of a young girl.

Further research conducted by the Alonzis concluded that the place was once a club, the Candlelight Lounge and that the second floor was used by prostitutes and hookers. Maybe the little girl belonged to one of the ladies of the evening? Maybe the ghost might go further back into history than that.

Update: Alonzi's Villa was recently demolished and no longer exists. It'll be interesting to see if anything happens on the spot of the new construction.

Hotel Baker
100 W. Main Street
St. Charles, IL. 60174
630-584-2100

According to local lore, a spirit haunts the historic St. Charles hotel where she was jilted on her wedding day 30 years ago. And the ghost of the young chambermaid who once worked at the Hotel Baker isn't the only specter in residence at the 1928-vintage, Spanish-Moroccan styled inn, some hotel staffers insist.

They swear they've also spotted a ghostly bell captain in an old-style formal uniform, walking the halls, and have been startled by a dapper gentleman, decked out in top hat and tails, frequenting a kitchen area that once was a banquet room and even occasionally feeling the tap of his cane.

"There are some employees who claim to have had some strange occurrences," said Craig Frank, a co-owner of the local landmark, which reopened as a luxury hotel in 1998 after years as a retirement home. There were $10 million in renovations.

A few unexplained visitors would only add to the already colorful history of the five-story landmark on the banks of the Fox River in downtown St. Charles, which entrepreneur Charles J. Baker (1868-1659) built using some of the $20 million he received from his heiress sister in the late 1910s.

Baker set out to build the "biggest small hotel." In 1926, Baker purchased the site of the old Haines Mill and hired Wolf, Sexton, Harper, and Trueax of St. Charles to design the hotel. The final design of the building blended the latest technology with Spanish Romantic Revival architecture. This style reflects the similar architectural style found across the Fox River on the Arcada Theater. Notable exterior features of the five-story building include: a square tower, a detailed center entrance with a unique combination of columns and a peacock-shaped stained glass window, gardens, terraces and a putting green.

Hotel Baker had the latest in modern conveniences from kitchen appliances to building elements. The structure of the building itself incorporated brick, concrete and steel-encased utilities, elements which made the building "fireproof." Instead of relying on outside services for electricity, Hotel Baker harnessed the power of the Fox River. Thanks to the use of this age-old method of energy production, the hotel avoided power outages, allowing guests to enjoy their stay in comfort.

Upon the opening celebration on June 2, 1928, three hundred and one guests caught their first glimpse of Baker's "pride and joy." Baker had spared no expense. In the end, the hotel cost approximately a million dollars. Not only were these early visitors treated to the splendor found throughout the public areas of the hotel, guests also could spend the night in one of the fifty-five custom designed rooms for $2.50. Also within the hotel were several shops: a women's clothing store, a newspaper shop, a barber, and a beauty shop. Adjacent to the hotel, there was a two-story parking garage and auto showroom.

While the hotel offered these conveniences and amenities to guests, the luxurious Rainbow and Trophy Rooms remained the highlights of one's visit. The Trophy Room, named for the number of trophies displayed, imitated a Spanish courtyard: balconies, awnings, a fountain and a simulated sky all contributed to the creation of this environment. The Rainbow Room, with its oval glass block floor and custom pipe organ, provided guests with a dazzling place to dance and dine. Until a 1955 flood, red, green, blue and amber lights beneath the floor created spectacular patterns. Unfortunately, following the flood, the lights could only be turned on and off.

He made the hotel a showplace, attracting well-heeled guests and big-name entertainers. Newlyweds came to stay at what was billed as the "Honeymoon Hotel." Bandleaders Guy Lombardo, Tommy Dorsey, Louis Armstrong and Lawrence Welk were among those who played the hotel's Rainbow Room in its heyday. Among those who visited the Baker Hotel were John F. Kennedy and Mayor Richard Daley.

After living on the fifth floor of the hotel for thirty-one years, Baker died in 1959 at the age of 90. Dellora Norris, Baker's niece, inherited the hotel. After she failed to sell the hotel, she gave it to the Lutheran Social Services of Illinois in 1968. Following some remodeling, the hotel reopened in 1971 as an interfaith, non-denominational residence for the elderly. Although the upper floors of the hotel were restricted to residents, the main public areas remained open for public use.

In 1996, Craig Frank and Neil Johnson, both St. Charles businessmen, bought the hotel. Following an extensive renovation, cleaning and upgrading of utilities, the hotel once again the "Crown Jewel of the Fox," welcomed guests offering them the latest in technology and luxury.

But one person who found no lasting happiness at the 55-room hotel was the young chambermaid, according to lore that has now gotten an international push with the inclusion of the hotel on a Website devoted to haunted hotels.

It's said she would sneak her lover into the sixth-floor employees' dormitory, where their sighs and moans occasionally could be heard.

Then, the young woman, who planned to be married in the hotel's Rose Garden, was supposedly jilted by her fiancé on their wedding day. Heartbroken, she threw herself into the Fox River, and her body was never recovered.

The history behind the legends may be suspect - several local historians don't recall a Fox River suicide like that described in the ghost story. But hotel staffers and guests still report hearing unsettling sighs and moans coming from the area that once housed the employees' rooms, Frank said.

He said he's never encountered anything supernatural there, "though I don't necessarily discount these stories. I believe there's a lot there we don't know about and can't understand."

Masked Ghost
Lombard, IL. 60148

Most people are perfectly content with Horatio's philosophy from Hamlet, Act I by William Shakespeare, "There are more things in heaven and earth, Horatio. Than are dreamt of in your philosophy." But those people obviously haven't made the acquaintance of the ghost in Sally's house.

Those few who have allegedly encountered the elusive apparition are convinced of its existence. To those who haven't, there remains the question, "To be or not to be" - regarding the ghost, that is.

Sally (not her real name) has since about 1976 lived in an allegedly haunted house in Lombard, Illinois. The house looks innocent enough. It is not even of those rambling monstrosities popular in the last century, where one might easily imagine a few spirits to roam. It is a compact, fairly small Cape Cod, about 53 years old, furnished in a modern style, and complete with a finished basement that has been converted into a recreation room with a bar.

Oddly enough, it is in that warm and cozy basement that spiritual manifestations are claimed to have been most pronounced.

The existence of Sally's ghost had become a subject of controversy among area parapsychologists and alleged psychics. Although none had actually seen it, some insist a "presence" is there, while others have found no evidence of it.

The ghost came into the limelight when Sally recently attended a lecture at the College of DuPage, Glen Ellyn, Illinois, by Dr. Jan Grossman. Grossman, a Philadelphia psychiatrist who investigates supernatural phenomena on the side, attests to the existence of a spirit world based on "unexplainable experiences" of his own.

Upon hearing Sally's account of the ghostly goings on, Grossman paid a visit to her home after the lecture. According to Sally and her 17-year-old baby sister, at the time, Grossman through a meditation technique, materialized the ghost.

The ghost was described as a face, appearing to wear a mask and a strange headdress that resembled a helmet. Although Grossman said he saw nothing, he claimed to have sensed a "presence" in the house. His wife, Susan, declined to comment on what she saw.

A visit to Sally's house by a Suburban Tribune reporter was said to have resulted in another appearance of the same face. Sally and her baby sitter again said they saw the face.

Sally's account of the apparition's antics is innumerable. With a tightening voice and eyes brimming with tears, she tells of her baby's crib being moved, objects disappearing from one place and reappearing in another, loud banging noises, footsteps, marks appearing on the walls, lamp globes shattering and finding uneaten meals that have been served put back in the refrigerator in Baggies.

Thinking she had a prowler, Sally has often summoned Lombard Police. Neither of two policemen questioned said he saw anything, but one said he heard the banging noise, "which might have been the furnace," and "saw the dog go bananas."

"Of course, it might have smelled another animal," Patrolman James Knicely said.

Taking her troubles to another field of investigation, Sally contacted parapsychologists Paul Palmer and Bobbie Joncas, both teachers at Richard J. Daley College in Chicago. With a team of investigators and equipment, Palmer and Joncas spent more than 40 hours in Sally's house, made photographic and sound tests, and thoroughly questioned all so-called witnesses.

They concluded that no ghost was present.

"We concede to a supernatural manifestation only after we have ruled out all rational explanations," Joncas said.

Palmer and Joncas said that questioning of witnesses revealed that none had actually seen any apparition.

Sally said she summoned a Catholic priest to exorcize the house. But saying there was no indication of a demon's presence, the priest would only bless the house, which Sally said had no effect on the apparition's annoying antics.

Upon Sally's request, alleged psychic Evelyn Paglini, director of the International Psychic Center, Elmhurst, Illinois, visited the house.

Before a gathering of reporters, photographers, and curious onlookers, including Palmer, Joncas, and their associate Frank Vondrak, all expecting to witness an exorcism, Paglini announced that she would conduct a séance instead, which apparently produced nothing other than a performance from Paglini.

Nobody, except Sally, saw any supernatural manifestation at the séance. Sally said she again saw the masked face, but only in a brief flash.

North Central College
30 N. Brainard Street
Naperville, IL. 60540
630-657-5100

North Central College was founded in 1861 by the Evangelical Association, a predecessor of the United Methodist Church. Until 1870, the college was located in Plainfield, Illinois, and was originally known as Plainfield College. The name was changed to North-Western College in 1864 and to North Central College in 1926.

The college's founders expressed the advanced thought for that day that "Christian commitment and intellectual attainments are compatible," and from the beginning the college was nonsectarian in it hiring and admission practices. This pioneering concept along with the commitment to inclusiveness and diversity that are hallmarks of the United Methodist Church is part of the heritage of North Central College and continues to add depth and meaning to its programs.

In 1870, the college moved to Naperville, Illinois, then an agricultural village of fewer than 2,000 people, located on the Burlington & Quincy railroad line. Today, Naperville is one of the fastest-growing and most desirable cities in the nation, with a population of more than 100,000 residents, outstanding community services and a reputation as the Midwest center of scientific research and development.

One student who attends North Central College in Naperville recently sent me an email regarding the alleged ghosts that haunt the campus buildings.

"I attend North Central College in Naperville (Illinois), and we have two buildings here that are supposedly haunted on campus. The first is Pfeiffer Hall (our main performance hall) is home to more than one ghost...according to students. I am skeptical to these stories since they are told by other students. It becomes hard to tell what would be trustworthy or not. However, there have been stories of faculty members seeing some pretty strange things. Pencils that are stolen by the ghost of a former music major who committed suicide (it is said he was working to become a composer), so on and so forth. There is another story told of a former director who had his children with him at the hall late one night, and when he went to go downstairs to get something, he told his children to come downstairs as the stairs were dangerous. His youngest child, a toddler at the time, was said to have fallen down the stairs and cracked its head open. I've had people tell me that this tragedy manifests in a toddler running around.

"The other supposedly haunted building, Seybert Hall, a dorm used primarily for incoming freshman. The story about this building includes a monk who walks around late at night. I have had a class in Pfeiffer, and haven't seen anything. However, I am not a music major, so I don't spend nearly as much time in that building as many others. Nor have I ever lived in Seybert Hall."

http://www.noctrl.edu/

Legends and Short Stories

Allerton Mansion
515 Old Timber Road
Monticello, IL. 61856
217-762-2721

Robert Henry Allerton was born on March 20, 1873, the only son of wealthy Chicagoan, Samuel Waters Allerton (1828-1914), and Pamilla Thompson Allerton (1840-1880). Samuel Allerton was a self-made man who made his millions in land, livestock, banking and other commercial enterprises.

The Allertons lived on Prairie Avenue, which in the 1800s was the most fashionable residential street in Chicago. They were neighbors of Marshall Fields, the Pullmans, the Kimballs, and the Armours. When Robert was a boy, Samuel had given him 280 acres of land in Piatt County. He also gave him the money to build a house on this land and the responsibility of managing the other Allerton land holdings in the same area. Robert named these holdings under his stewardship "The Farms." By 1914, "The Farms" consisted of about 12,000 acres which Robert had acquired through inheritance, purchase and trade.

In 1946 Robert gave part of "The Farms" to the University of Illinois. He stipulated that "it was to be used by the University as an educational and research center, as a forest and wild-life and plant-life preserve, as an example of landscape architecture, and as a public park. The portion known as the Woodland Property, approximately 1,500 acres in extent, has been named Robert Allerton Park...(another) area consisting of 3,775 acres of land in eight different farms lying north of the Sangamon River, was provided with the stipulation that its income be used to maintain and develop the Park."

Robert Henry Allerton died on December 22, 1964 at the age of ninety-one. At his request, his body was cremated and the ashes were scattered on the outgoing tide in the bay at Lawai-Kai. There was no memorial service. He left us, his public benefactors, living memorials in Allerton Gardens, Kaui, the Honolulu Academy of Art, the Art Institute of Chicago, and Robert Allerton Park.

There have been reports of a mysterious lady in white. She, according to witnesses and old photographs of people that use to go there as a guest of Robert Allerton, is a guest that frequently visited here. She has been seen walking along the pond in the back of the mansion and in her room trying on hats and gloves. She's been heard coming down the stairs and pacing the hall in front of her room.

Others have just noted a strange feeling in the air while visiting the gardens and the mansion itself.

Billy Goat Tavern
430 N. Michigan Avenue
Chicago, IL. 60611
312-222-1525

Wheaton comedian John Belushi brought the Bill Goat national fame when he portrayed a frenzied Greek cook on "Saturday Night Live" in the mid-'70s. But the Bill Goat, located out of the light of day on murky Lower Michigan Avenue, had long been a local legend, since original owner William Sianis was forbidden by Chicago Cubs management to bring his house goat into Wrigley Field during a 1945 World Series game between the Chicago Cubs and Detroit Tigers. Current Cubs owner, at the time, P.K. Wrigley, was quoted as saying, "Don't bring that goat in here. That goat smells."

Insulted, Sianis' curse that the Cubs would never again win a championship has held true. The Bill Goat, founded across the street from the old Chicago Stadium on Madison Street in 1934 and relocated to Michigan Avenue in 1964, also is known for its collection of newspapermen who wandered in after their dailies were put to bed. Eminent Chicago writers such as Dave Condon, Mike Royko, Irv Kupicnet, Bill Granger and Roger Ebert are honored with blown-up bylines plastered behind one length of the L-shaped bar and on the "Wall of Fame" of pictures and articles on the other side of the room. Some still frequent the place, which has a central grill in between two dining areas, with a "VIP Room" sequestered to the rear.

"Reporters like it down here because it's old-fashioned," said Bill Sianis, son of Sam Sianis, the founder's nephew and current owner. The Bill Goat reeks with local color; pictures, news clippings and trivia including numerous tributes to William Sianis after his passing in 1970, a "Wise Guys Corner" of Chicago crooks and a decree from the Chicago Police Department. That's Sam himself doing a Greek dance, pictured behind the bar under the wall clock. He's also photographed schmoozing with various Greek beauty queens.

Sam has tried to remove the curse himself by attempting to bring a goat to a Cubs game back in 1973 but the goat was not allowed inside. However, in 1984 and again in 1989, Cubs management invited the goat to opening day festivities and while the Cubs luck did change for a bit, it seems the curse is still rooted into the north side ball park.

When the original goat died, he was stuffed by a taxidermist and kept at the original bar then located on Madison Avenue. After the assassination of Dr. Martin Luther King and the riots that followed in 1968, the tavern was engulfed in flames along with the goat. To placate the original goat perhaps another stuffed goat now resides at it's Michigan Avenue location. Another Bill Goat is scheduled to be unveiled at Navy Pier in Chicago very soon.

http://www.billygoattavern.com/home.html

The Bleeding Stop Sign
Riverside Road at Olmsted
Riverside, IL. 60546

Sometimes inanimate objects appear to display a life of their own or even exude bodily fluids, even blood! Such alleges to be the case at The Bleeding Stop Sign in Riverside where supposedly a tragic accident occurred in July of 1967 when a teenager was killed here apparently while drag racing another car. Through the 1960s and 1970s, legends began to spring up that blood would occasionally appear on the stop sign or what appeared to be blood. Not many were willing or daring enough to actually approach the phantom goo and discover what it really was.

Perhaps this substance is a constant reminder to others to slow down and live? Or is it the work of pranksters who periodically splatter ordinary ketchup on the sign? Those who live in the area around Riverside, Lyons, North Riverside and Brookfield truly believe that something supernatural is happening here. I suppose the mystery could be solved by actually collecting a sample of the spectral fluid for analysis, if in fact the story is really true. There have been a number of other deaths associated with that intersection since the

1967 accident that seems to have precipitated the legend. Perhaps there is some truth to the story and maybe, just maybe, the sign is acting as a warning to others of future generations.

Chodl Auditorium
Morton East High School
2423 S. Austin Blvd.
Cicero, IL. 60804

A teacher/director is said to haunt the theater. According to legend, he died of a heart attack the opening night of West Side Story and never got to see the production. Students have claimed to see and feel a presence in theater especially later at night after long rehearsals. West Side Story hasn't been put on out of respect but once since his death.

Chodl Auditorium was named after the father of a local dentist. The teacher who allegedly died in the theater isn't traceable so it may in fact be just an urban legend spun by each class of students who attend the school. However, theaters in general have always been good places for ghosts to manifest. Such was the case Morton College, Oak Park/River Forest High School and even the Woodstock Opera House, all mentioned in Windy City Ghosts.

http://mortontheatre.tripod.com/Chodl_Auditorium/chodl_auditorium.html

Cook County Jail
2700 S. California Avenue
Chicago, IL. 60608
773-869-7100

In 1928, construction was started on this current facility at 26th and California, next door to the city's House of Corrections. The new structure was finished by the end of the next year, and the adjoining Criminal Courthouse was completed soon after. The new County jail and neighboring House of Corrections had a combined daily population of more than 3200 inmates, which was then believed to be the largest concentration of prisoners in the free world.

Throughout the 1930s and '40s, both the County Jail and House of Corrections met the challenge of overcrowding with some success. But by the mid 1950s the problem became overwhelming. The jail was often occupied by as many as 2400 inmates a day, twice its designated capacity. Management of the jail's population was made more difficult by the presence of a large number of sentenced inmates who were previously shipped to the state prison system to serve their terms but were now being sentenced to time in the County Jail.

In 1929, only 7 percent of the Jail's population was sentenced, while 93 percent were being held temporarily pending the outcome of their trials. By 1954, nearly 60% of the Jail's daily population had been sentenced to terms as long as five years. The county had the additional burden of conducting executions, which was traditionally a state function, and maintaining a death row for those inmates awaiting their date with the County Jail's electric chair.

As conditions at the County Jail continued to deteriorate, several community leaders and elected officials called for reforms in the county criminal justice system. In 1969, the Illinois State Legislature finally acted. They voted into law a statue that created the Cook County Department of Corrections which combined the County Jail and the city's House of Corrections under one authority. Though the two facilities stood side-by-side at 26th and California and performed virtually the same tasks, they were run separately for more than 40 years. When the DOC was formed, staff and inmate populations from both facilities were combined to form one correctional institution.

Over the next 20 years, the DOC's chief concern was dealing with the never ending problem of overcrowding. Spurred by a series of federal court orders to relieve crowding, the DOC oversaw the construction of several new jail builds.

Today the DOC administers eleven separate jail divisions, house nearly 9000 inmates and employs more than 3000 correctional offices and support staff. Though overcrowding is still a problem, the DOC, under the direction of County Sheriff Michael F. Sheahan, had developed a series alternative program. In 1993, Sheahan created the Department of Community Supervision and Intervention (DCSI), which takes non-violent jail inmates and places them in programs where they receive drug rehabilitation, high school equivalency courses and job training.

There seems to be a series of unusual things associated with a particular jail cell. Apparently most of the suicides have taken place in one jail cell. A Chicago Tribune reporter attempted to gather some information as to why this might be the case. Was there perhaps one incident that had started this? The rumor is that is was the jail cell of mass murderer Richard Speck who killed eight student nurses on July 13, 1966.

He forced his way into the nurses' townhouse at 2319 E. 100th Street. Only 23-year-old Corazon Amurao escaped by rolling underneath a bunk bed. She would be the one to positively identify Speck as the suspect. Speck avoided arrest for a number of days until he attempted to slash his wrists and was taken to a hospital, where he was recognized as the mass murderer.

He was sentenced to the electric chair; he was resentenced to eight consecutive terms of 50 to 150 years. Facing a possible total of 1200 years in prison, Speck seemed to have received the longest sentence in history. By 1976, however, he was eligible for parole, and although turned down, he was entitled to a review of his case each year thereafter.

Speck died at 6:05 a.m. on December 6, 1991 in Silver Cross Hospital in Joliet after suffering a massive heart attack. Speck's heart weighed 690 grams, while a normal heart for a man his age, 49, would weigh 400 grams, Will County Coroner, Duane A. Krieger said.

The townhouse where the murders took place did seem to have a series of bad luck for awhile. The blood stains were not immediately removed and blood, once it sets in wood, is extremely hard, if not impossible, to remove. The townhouse went through a series of changes. For awhile it was used as a half-way house for drug rehabilitation. Those people in the drug treatment programs often claimed that there were ghostly things going on in the building. However, they aren't necessarily the best witnesses in the world.

A woman living right next door started experiencing some strange hallucinations, or so she thought. She imagined she heard the screams and sounds constantly coming thorough the walls and wasn't sure if they were simply in her own head. The sounds were coming from the area where the murders took place even though it was currently empty and unoccupied at the time.

Elgin State Hospital Cemetery
Off Route 20
Elgin, IL. 60120

There have been several reports of cruel treatment to the inmates at Elgin State Hospital for years, even those of radioactive tests on humans during the mid-century. The cemetery is a little far from the campus of buildings. There is no sign, only a gate that barely bars entrance. It is alleged that there is a grave where five bodies are buried under a single name.

People have reported orbs and full-bodied

apparitions here throughout the years. Though the cemetery is inactive in terms of burial, it isn't closed to the public. As nearby construction is taking place, I can only imagine ghost activity on the rise.

http://elginpostcards.tripod.com/elginstatehospitalannex.htm

The Gate
Rt. 137, near Independence Grove Forest Preserve
Libertyville, IL. 60048

In a small clearing in the far northern suburbs is where a small school house used to stand, according to legend. The house was torn down years ago. All that remains is a huge, black iron gate. Legend has it that a lunatic broke into the school one day and killed all of the children, decapitating some of them in the process. It is further told that, with the disembodied heads in hand; he walked over to the gate and staked their heads on the sharp

points of the fence.

The community decided to raze the structure after this event, but The Gate still remains as a memory. It's told that you can still hear children crying and see their heads on the gate every now and then. It is also said that, even if you don't know the story, looking at The Gate can produce an overwhelming sense of grief in the onlooker.

However, this author wasn't able to trace this story or the tragic events beyond folk tales and legends. Is it true or the product of a vivid story-teller and the story being handed down from one generation to the next?

What can be said of the legend that is true is that at one point in time the land behind the gate did serve as a camp. The St. Francis Boys Camp opened for operation sometime after 1950. Before that it was used as the Katherine Dodridge Kreigh Budd Memorial Home for Children. This orphanage for over 100 children opened in 1925.

The stories don't end there either. There are additional stories regarding the houses that stand across the street from this north side landmark. An easily dismissible, but strangely well-known fallacy is that the neighborhood is full of devil worshippers. However wild and random these claims are, several more reputable stories have been told about the area.

Several people in the area have made the statement that they are sharing their homes with past residents who move about in shadowy forms. Hunters in the area have come across nearby farms only to see phantoms of long deceased gangsters from the 1930s.

Hitchhiking Nun
Chicago, IL.

This tale takes place in Chicago in December of 1941 just after the Japanese sneak attack on Pearl Harbor, Hawaii. A local cab driver was driving around the downtown area with visions of a fare dancing in his head, as there were numerous last-minute Christmas shoppers still roaming the streets. Much to his surprise, he saw a nun near a curb who apparently wished to use his services that evening.

She jumped in, glad to be out of the cold and swirling snowflakes which were beginning to come down heavy. The nun gave the cabby an address which he knew as a rather lonely, isolated locale in the far southwestern suburbs. Knowing this would be a nice fair and perhaps looking forward to a nice tip, he pulled away from the curb and they started on their way.

They talked together about the upcoming Christmas season and, of course, Pearl Harbor when she suddenly directed him to turn onto a dark, deserted road. He was taken aback and almost missed the turn as it wasn't well marked and partially hidden by shrubbery. The path eventually led to a large stone building. As he pulled over to the building, which he sure was her final destination, she was nowhere to be found! The backseat was completely empty and the nun was gone!

Trembling from fright, he decided to pull up to the building which was a convent. He knocked on the massive door and was greeted by several more sisters who ushered him inside once she saw how frightened the man looked.

Inside the convent a wall was covered with pictures of nuns and sisters, and as he told his strange tale to the Mother Superior, he happened to glance up at one of the pictures and immediately recognized his lost fare. "That's her!" he almost shouted. "She's the person that I drove here tonight."

The Mother Superior cast a look at the picture the cabby was pointing to and exclaimed that that was impossible. You see that nun had died almost ten years earlier, had wanted to come home and apparently did just that that snowy evening.

The Glowing Tombstone
St. Peter & Paul Cemetery
Columbia & North Streets
Naperville, IL. 60540

    In St. Peter and Paul Cemetery, located in DuPage County, a favorite past time for local youths was to drive along the frontage of the graveyard and look for the glowing tombstone. According to locals, the stone would suddenly, without warning, glow a brilliant orange and quickly die out before the vehicle could be stopped. While there were indeed other stones on the hill, it appeared that only one would give off this ethereal glow. What could be the cause?

    The explanation was quite simple and not at all paranormal. It seems that about four or five years ago, the town of Naperville installed some very bright orange, mercury vapor lamps and that's approximately when the legend "came to life." The lamps give off a very distinctive orange glow and the tombstone in question is lined up just perfectly to reflect the light from the street lamp. The others are either not perfectly aligned or do not have highly reflective surfaces like the glowing tombstone. Neighboring stones are carved from rough marble while the glowing stone has a highly polished surface. Mystery solved!

Leland Hotel
7 S. Stolp Avenue
Aurora, IL. 60506
630-897-6055

The Leland Hotel when completed in 1928 was the tallest building outside of Chicago at 22 stories. The architecture features Italian Romanesque styling popular at the time. The top floor Sky Club ballroom, built in 1937, was a famous venue for blue performance and recordings. It was there that some of the early legends of the Blues like Tampa Red and Big Joe Williams. "Sonny Boy" Williamson, recorded for the Bluebird label (the reason being, that the record company could get non-union engineers out there and by-pass the need to have to pay the union scale wages of Chicago.) The building was designed by Anker Sveere Graven and Arthur Guy Mayger of Chicago.

Now known at the Fox Island Place, it is used for apartments and office space. According to local legend, a number of suicides have taken place by guests jumping from upper floors into the Fox River. At night obnoxious odors seem to drift from the bank of elevators while strange moaning sounds also emanate from the closed elevator doors.

Maxwell Street Ghost
Chicago, IL.

Over the last two decades, several sightings of a Lady in Black have been reported in area around Maxwell Street in Chicago. This historic area was just southwest of the Loop, by the University of Illinois at Chicago campus. Its center was as South Halsted Street and Maxwell Street. Halsted is a main (North-South) arterial street and Maxwell is just two blocks south of Roosevelt Road, a main east-west Street. The Greek town and Little Italy neighborhoods were nearby.

In September of 1994, the Maxwell Street Market in Chicago was destroyed by the City of Chicago and the University of Illinois at Chicago. That old Maxwell Street Market was, in the opinion of many, the greatest outdoor urban bazaar ever - - mammoth, diverse, exciting, historical, great food and a place where all ethnic and racial groups got along. The old market did have problems but rather than solve them, the market was destroyed.

The encounters have always taken place outdoors, and the good-Samaritan spirit appears to want to help people or warn them. One report dates back to 1969.

"I was 20-years-old. I was enrolled in the Chicago Police Academy, which was located near Maxwell Street and the Dan Ryan Expressway. I had been attending the academy for several months and was taking lunch with two other academy students. As we entered a small restaurant in the area, I remember a white lady dressed in all black clothes. Her dress reminded me of someone from the 1800s, and the reason I mentioned her color is because the area was basically a black neighborhood and seeing a white lady in this area made this individual encounter even stranger.

"Now, as I stood in the entryway to the restaurant with my friends on either side of me, this Lady in Black came up to me and looked right into my eyes. Without a word or hand gesture or even a facial expression, she somehow communicated to me to hand her the pen and small note pad I had in my upper left-hand shirt pocket. I did just that without knowing exactly why. She took the pen and note pad and wrote something. Then she looked at me and shook her head in a gesture of no, no, no. She handed me the pen and note pad and left abruptly. I looked at the note pad and noticed what she wrote: my name and birth date. But then I also realized that it was in my own handwriting.

"I quickly turned to my friends and asked them, 'Did you see what the lady just did?' They responded to my question as though I was crazy. 'What lady?' They acted as if nothing unusual happened, and we went into the restaurant and had lunch.

"Well, this strange little encounter stayed with me and I always felt that I would have to quit the Chicago Police Department someday. I felt she was telling me to leave this career option in order to save my life. Now, I never told many people of this story. However, I saw a TV show (Unsolved Mysteries) in which a Lady in Black had saved a motorcyclist on a highway near this area in Chicago and how paramedics and others saw this Lady in Black come to his aid and save his life. I am now certain that it was the same Lady in Black I encountered outside that Maxwell Street restaurant."

Mt. Olivet Cemetery
278 Ashland Avenue
Aurora, IL. 60505
630-897-9250

Mount Olivet Cemetery in Kane County, Aurora, Illinois is operated by Catholic Cemeteries and is allegedly haunted by women seen dressed in 1950s clothing sometimes standing by a 1958 Lincoln Continental. They seem to melt and fade away when viewed.

Warren Park
5631 W. 16th Street
Cicero, IL. 60804

Inside the Warren Park Administration Building, on the top floor, people have heard what sounds like moaning and groaning and phantom footsteps, always after hours. An actual sighting of a misty apparition has been witnessed plus doors opening. There is also a report on record of a glass window being totally shattered under mysterious circumstances.

A couple of years ago a young child was killed in a gang-related drive-by shooting at the park. Perhaps his ghost is one of the apparitions seen in the area. Untimely death is often a scenario that is retold concerning reports of ghosts. Usually the ghost is simply that of a residual haunting due to the trauma and suddenness of the death. This could be the case at Warren Park.

Willow Springs Fire Station #1
Willow Springs, IL. 60480

In 1892 the city water works began installing water lines on First Street. The project was completed in 1894. That same year the water and fire company responded to the Snelson & Lovan Saloon, located on First Street, to extinguish a fire. This was the first recorded fire call in Willow Springs.

The first fire station was located on the corner of First Street and Pine Grove Road, in a portion of the Grant Davis Lumber Company Building. In later years, the city built another fire station on Second Street, located in once was the Police Department. During that time period it was in the front section of City Hall.

One of the spirits that is supposed to have made her presence known is of very recent times. The spirit of Diane Masters is said to have occupied the Willow Springs Fire Station No. 1 for a while.

After recovering the vehicle containing her corpse from the Ship and Sanitary

Canal, it was temporarily stored in the firehouse pending investigation and disposal by the authorities. Periodically the station lights would turn on or the siren would go off with no reasonable explanation. This continued from time to time until the arrest and conviction of those said to be responsible for her death. Her spirit is apparently at rest now and strange things are no longer happening at the fire station.

Zion Cemetery
Zion, IL. 60099

A gravestone in this cemetery is often visited by local teenagers as they say it gives off a strange blue light that once you approach it, it disappears from sight. It is often encountered on dark nights where no moon is out and can sometimes be observed in a church just down the road as well.

A phantom car is also seen on a Fulton County back road called Babylon, just off of county highway 17 going east. The origin of this car and the light are total mysteries as there isn't much researchable information or witnesses that have claimed to have observed either first-hand.

Haunted Houses

A hungry Boy?

An acquaintance of mine used to live in what she believed to be a haunted abode. Here is her story, in her own words.

"We used to live in an apartment that we think might have been haunted. If it was, it was by two different spirits, or whatever you want to call them. I used to catch, every now and then, the figure of a small boy standing beside my refrigerator. He never ventured farther than the kitchen and I never felt any fear when I saw him, and he was usually gone so fast that you weren't even sure what you saw.

"I never said anything to my husband or neighbors because I thought they would think I was a nut case! One evening one of my friends and I were playing cards in the kitchen and she looked up and said one of the kids was awake. I went and checked but they were both sound asleep. She had glimpsed this spirit and thought it was one of mine!

"One morning my husband was telling me that during the night he woke up to find a kid standing in the kitchen and staring into our bedroom but he never moved towards us. Dave (her husband) watched him for a little while and then he just disappeared! That's when I knew I wasn't crazy after all and I told him about all the times I had seen this child also.

"The other thing that I always felt, but never saw, thank God, was a feeling of intense fear in the back bedroom. There were times that I would literally run from the room because I knew if I turned around, something would be there, but I also knew it wouldn't be that little boy.

"The feeling of fear would be so intense in the back bedroom where the kids slept and I could feel it in other parts of the apartment, but it was strongest in that bedroom. I hated to be there after dark and even during daylight, I was uneasy. My husband never felt like that though my oldest daughter did. At the time she was three-years-old, she would wake up many nights screaming about the 'shadows,' as she would say. We tried night lights, but that never helped. At the time we thought it was just a childhood fear of the dark.

"Sometimes I would be at a neighbor's apartment until after dark and when I went home, as soon as I put my hand on the doorknob to open the front door, I would get this feeling so strongly that when I opened the door; something was on the other side waiting for me. Now, I'm not a nervous type, but that place really bothered me. I couldn't sit in that apartment in the dark watching TV. I had to keep lights on. I've never had a problem before we lived there, or after we lived there. Even now, I turn off all the lights in the house when watching TV. In my current home, I'm not afraid anywhere....nothing bothers me....but in that one apartment, I was afraid all the time, but never when I saw the child standing there. Funny thing is, I never saw him anywhere but the kitchen, nowhere else in the place. The back bedroom where the kids slept was right off the kitchen but I never saw him in there; just the kitchen.

Danaka Faye's House
Chicago, IL.

Once in a great while or even once in a lifetime, a researcher might just run across a truly haunted house that displays all the earmarks of the classic haunting and produces some physical proof in the form of photographs, video and audio tape. Such was the case at Danaka's house located not far from the intersection of Belmont and Harlem on the north side. Only her first name and vague location will be used in the telling of this most unusual and ongoing investigation.

On July 30, 1998, I received a Fax which read: "I found your web sight today and had to get in touch with you. I really want to talk to someone about my home in Chicago. I just know a spirit is there. I have seen him on two occasions, both at night in my bedroom doorway. One night I was terrified when I suddenly woke up (I have no clue why) and my husband was saying Andrew. This was really strange because we have been married for two years and he has never talked in his sleep. Nor has he said anything since then. I was reading your guest book and realized I have a spirit. Could you please contact me?"

As you might imagine, I get a lot of calls, faxes and emails from people all across the world everyday telling me about the same kind of story. While many are out-of-state and difficult to help over the phone or through the Internet, this one was local and sounded very interesting. I immediately contacted Danaka the next day and through a telephone conversation was convinced that she wasn't crazy or imagining these strange events. It became quite apparent that something spooky indeed was happening in her home.

They had lived there for about two and a half years before strange things began to happen in June of 1996. The home was built around 1925 and been through numerous owners and tenants as it became apparent that no one could or would live there for very long.

The first episodes were low-level and hardly worth telling until much more began to happen further on down the line. Danaka would constantly see movements out of the corner of her eyes and when she would turn in that direction, nothing would be there. Other times she told of writing checks at the kitchen table only to see someone or something pass in front of her. Thinking it was her husband, she would look up instantly and, of course, emptiness would greet her.

Objects of a personal nature would become lost or displaced for weeks at a time and would later turn up in the most obvious of places without a satisfactory explanation of how they turned up there. Her cat and dog both would react strangely in different ways. The dog would bark at the empty staircase leading to the upstairs bedrooms even though nobody was up there at the time. While the cat would apparently follow something across the living room with her eyes and even seemed to be playing with an unseen playmate during one particular episode. Peanut, the cat, would sometimes swat at something invisible to Danaka while sitting on the couch in the living room.

The straw that broke the camel's back was the very frightening nighttime apparition that appeared in her bedroom doorway one evening. She described him as male, with short hair and a blue uniform. He was just leaning against the doorway, grinning at her! Danaka turned over, rubbed her eyes and looked again. He was still there. He then began to dissolve away very slowly.

Another time Danaka recalled the feeling of someone pulling on her legs in the middle of the night and screaming in her ears! Yet nobody was there and her husband, Ken, never woke up.

She would sometimes feel the end of the bed depress as though a person had just sat at the edge. Ken began talking in his sleep and calling out the name, Andrew, which they don't know anyone with that name. Bathroom lights would begin to flicker and then turn themselves off and on without human assistance.

In September of 1998, an investigative team was assembled and told absolutely nothing about the case whatsoever. While using hand-held devices, they soon discovered that the meters indicated the upstairs as the hot-spots of activity. Exactly where Danaka had seen her uniformed apparition!

The entire upstairs was wired with equipment including Sony night vision cameras, RF modulators, coaxial cable and television monitors to observe the upstairs in real time. Tri-Field Meters, Geiger-Counter, Negative Ion Detector and a FM Transmitter linked to a Oscilloscope was used to detect unusual sounds which were recorded on a tape recorder.

After the video tapes were reviewed, I got quite a shock! There were numerous orbs or floating lights that the night vision cameras had captured. The first one was and still is the most amazing image ever recorded there or anywhere for that matter. Two night vision cameras were piggy-backed to watch both bedrooms at opposite ends of the hallway. In the hallway and doorway where Danaka's eerie encounter occurred, a bright, pulsing rectangular-shaped object appeared to emerge from the hallway wall, float in a most unusual manner upwards into Danaka's bedroom and disappear! It was a truly amazing image!

There were a number of other similar images floating down the door jam in a vertical trajectory before mysteriously disappearing. We obviously were onto something here. During a number of subsequent follow-up investigations with additional equipment and cameras, it became quite apparent that these orbs were a supernatural manifestation and not dust particles, insects or light reflections. The orbs zigzagged, most times defying gravity while other times glowing, changing luminosity and whizzing past both fast and extremely slow.

In July of 1999, Michael Hoff Productions wanted to shoot a segment in the house for the Discovery Channel. Danaka agreed to tell her story to the world while we would attempt to recreate the events that transpired during our numerous investigations. Investigators Stanley Suho, John Cachel, Jim Graczyk, Howard Hight and I were selected to set up the massive amount of equipment necessary to conduct a proper investigation.

The air-conditioning had to be turned off for audio production purposes and it soon became unbearably hot in the downstairs kitchen where the command post was set up. For well over an hour, nothing transpired but suddenly the unexpected happened.

While the group was all watching the monitors for orbs and motion, strange unexplained sounds began to emanate from the upstairs. Sounds that were growing louder by the minute. The noises resembled the shuffling of feet on the hardwood floors and metallic objects being dropped or moved around the empty rooms! The monitors clearly showed that no one, human that is, was upstairs at the time. I immediately sent Graczyk upstairs to search for a source to the sounds.

A window was open in the room but there were no metal blinds that could have caused the sounds. While upstairs Graczyk was instructed to shuffle his feet around to see if the sounds heard moments ago were similar to human footfalls. They matched almost identically! A professional wireless microphone was left in the suspect room by the sound man of the production crew. The window was closed and the upstairs again completely closed off.

Within a few minutes, the sounds started up again and they were most definitely within the confines of the room itself and not from outside. Then the orbs were observed. A number of them were seen by all in real time in both the upstairs bedrooms. The orbs were either self-illuminated or were lit up by the infrared illuminators on the night vision cameras.

After a lull in the action, a number of the team was sent upstairs to check on the status of video tapes and batteries when the orbs began to interact with the team members. In the totally pitch black bedrooms, the investigators had trouble seeing their hands in front of their faces however the orbs were clearly visible to the others at the command post but not to those stationed upstairs. After awhile the phenomena ceased altogether.

Later the tapes were analyzed and no clear source to this day was the culprit for the unusual metallic sounds. There was nothing upstairs in either bedroom that could have produced the strange sounds heard by all that evening.

It is the author's opinion that the genuine thing is happening at Danaka's house and more ongoing investigations are necessary to determine the possible cause or personalities of the haunters of her property. Danaka, however, takes all of this in stride and is not a bit afraid of sharing her home with a ghost or ghosts.

Is Anyone There?
83rd & Langley
Chicago, IL. 60619

Even though it was early May of 1982, there was still a slight chill in the air as we approached the collection of apartment complexes in the south side of Chicago. The snow had already melted and the grass was beginning to show the first signs of the life of Spring. The apartment buildings looked ordinary enough; almost too ordinary and innocent, but within one apartment lurked something sinister, something not of this world.

I remember the first conversation that I had with Pat Shenberg, (at that time the President of the Illinois Society of Psychic Research), concerning this dwelling, its residents and the strange occurrences that were reported within. The women involved in this strange episode and first haunted house case that I investigated professionally will be called Marsha (to protect her privacy) and her daughter, Nancy.

Shenberg told of the many unusual events that had been reported during the past seven years; many that defied natural known explanations. Objects would appear and then disappear directly in plain view of the occupants. Known in the vernacular as "apports", they would be seen by both women at the same time occasionally. There were also strange rapping and knocking sounds coming from within the walls of the apartment, reminiscent of poltergeist-type cases. However she did not believe this to be the case, as the age of the women precluded this possible conclusion.

Because there were no adolescents or children involved in this case, we ruled out the possibility for the moment and also based that on some of the other types of phenomena that had been reported.

Strange psychic music was heard, stemming from the bathroom even though no radios or TVs were left on unattended. Electrical appliances were affected and kitchen utensils were often found in very strange places. The refrigerator was occasionally found in shambles with eggs broken, bacon strips hanging from the inside shelves and other contents strewn about.

The kitchen drawers were also the victims of psychic foul-play. On several occasions they were found pulled out and the contents rearranged haphazardly. Marsha, herself, was also being physically attacked by something that she couldn't see but only feel. Strange burning sensations ravished her entire left side of her body and personal effects, such as nylons and hair curlers, were being destroyed or simply hidden from sight; only weeks later to be discovered in very obvious locations.

Besides this, there was allegedly physical proof of the existence of something supernatural. Coins, in the form of nickels and dimes mysteriously appeared out of nowhere and dropped to the ground and excrement was also discovered in Marsha's bed on one occasion.

This sounded like a very interesting but disturbing case, and as we approached the front door of the apartment, I couldn't help but feel that something was watching us from the darkened windows above. This was the first time that I had this strange feeling and it was not a comfortable feeling.

Various cameras were employed including two 35mm SLR camera. One loaded with 400 ASA color slide film and the other was equipped with color infrared film which was pushed to 400 ASA. Two portable tape recorders were used, one to record normal conversations and our interview of the residents and the other to perhaps pick up any odd sounds or disturbances in the other rooms including any electronic voice phenomena (EVP). A camcorder was also used and focused on the room where most of the activity was reported in the past.

Burdened down with all this equipment, we climbed the stairs to the third floor and knocked on the door. An elderly well-dressed Black woman opened the door and bade us to come in.

The apartment's interior was immaculate and well furnished. Everything was in perfect order with absolutely nothing out-of-place. The warm, friendly greeting that we received at the door temporarily made us forget why we were there in the first place. How could a beautifully kept up apartment with a kindly old lady and her daughter be haunted? We later found out that Nancy only began to room there with her mother after the phenomena became so terrifying that she did not wish to be alone anymore.

Marsha was 77, although she didn't look a day over 60 and Nancy was her 47-year-old daughter, who sort of became a permanent house-guest for the time being.

Marsha then began to tell us some of the unusual events that had taken place over the years. "It started along in December. The first thing that I noticed but didn't pay no attention to - I was smoking in my bedroom near a little table. I set the ashtray on the side of the bed and then went to the bathroom. When I came back, the ashes were on the television.

"A few nights after that, it happened again but I still didn't think anything about it. I pin curler my hair at night and when I finished, I looked down and part of the pin curler box was gone! I got down on the floor and stuck my hand around under the couch, looking for it. The next morning, I was folding up the covers and took two pillows off the couch and the top of the box was inside one pillow!"

Nancy was witness to many events that happened too but her attitude was completely different from that of her mother.

"Weird things happen with me but my reaction - it's hilariously funny even though it's weird. I walked in the kitchen one night. I have a habit of eating at night and pulled out the drawer where the knives and forks are and there was a clean plate there sitting on top of the silverware. The next day I went in the bathroom to brush my teeth. I tried to open the toothpaste tube but no matter how I tried, it wouldn't open. I thought I'd give it one more try, and wrenched at it with all my might and felt like a fool, 'cause the thing opened right away.

"Something weird happened in my room," recalled Nancy, "I was lying one night in bed; she (Marsha) was asleep. I got up to use the bathroom and when I got to the door something hit the floor. Ping! I looked and it's a quarter. Of course, she woke up. She said, 'What was that?' I said, 'There was a quarter somewhere in the bed because it stuck to me and fell off.' I went back to bed, got up later and it happened again the same night in the same spot. Dull thuds also started. It starts in the middle of one wall and continues to the middle of another directly behind the couch."

"Wait a minute," Shenberg says, "are your cameras ready? She has something behind her. On the left side. I don't know if it will stay there or not. Don't move because if you do, it will move with you. We're filming something behind you. There's a light behind her and I suspect that the light is what I call an essence of spirit."

I snapped off several frames with each camera aimed in the direction that Pat indicated, based on what she was seeing clairvoyantly. When the pictures were developed a few days later, it showed nothing unusual on the high-speed film, but on the infrared, exactly where Shenberg said she saw a light, were diagonal streaks of red light! This was proof enough for me that Shenberg was indeed seeing something that was there but totally invisible to the naked eye.

Shenberg goes into a deeper self-induced trance and begins to describe the man that she is seeing. "I see a little grey here in front. He was not a big man. Seems like he's a little darker than Nancy. The man that I see may have been inclined to wear a strange pin-stripped or patterned vest type thing. I also sense music around him. Either he like or played music."

"He was a musician," Nancy exclaimed, "I didn't think about that but he played a flute. He played in a band."

The pieces of the puzzle now began to fall into place. The knocking and rapping sounds were the first evidence of spirit contact as the ghost was trying to communicate and gain recognition. The psychic music was the flute that her deceased husband used to play when he was alive. They separated several years ago and he died during the separation.

Apparently he was coming back and trying to get a message across to both of them. The money could symbolize an unclaimed will or actual monies left behind by the deceased that was never recovered.

The other incidents such as the refrigerator, drawers and utensils could be a sign that because of Marsha's decision not to have anything to do with the ghost inhabiting the house, he possibly became more agitated and began to cause physical destruction to get his point across.

Shenberg suggested that they should look for a possible will or money left behind and also to totally forgive him for all his shortcomings in life. This way there would be nothing for him to hand onto.

One unusual event worth mentioning occurred about a half-hour after our arrival. While we were interviewing the couple, I noticed a strange heaviness in my chest and lungs that couldn't be attributed to a stuffy or humid day. It overtook me rapidly and made me very uncomfortable. Later, while we were discussing how her husband died, we discovered that he had been a very heavy smoker of cigars and cigarettes and had indeed died of lung cancer. Was this some kind of psychic feedback or impression that I received while sitting in the living room? Or was it just some little bit of edginess from the case in general?

Shenberg performed a general healing on Marsha and vowed that these occurrences would soon cease and dissipate forever. We had since contacted Marsha and Nancy to inquire if they had any further problems and were told that the manifestations had ceased rather abruptly and that everything was completely normal and serene.

Apparently her husband's ghost just wanted to get his message across which he did, after which he departed peacefully into the light of the spirit world.

Valerie Kolacki Apartment
Justice, IL. 60458

An apartment complex built in 1961 seemed to house its share of spirits according to Valerie Kolacki when she contacted me in August of 1995. Within shouting distance of nearby Bethania Cemetery, consecrated in 1894, this strange triangular-shaped area of land had tombstones in the back yard, one of which had fallen over on its side and was partially obscured with bushes. At first, Valerie simply thought that they were discarded concrete slabs until her niece began to move some dirt away from the larger one and discovered some writing. After I was invited to investigate the site, I dug a bit deeper and was amazed to find written on the tombstone the following: "August Boness, GEB 15 Oct 1888, GEST 26 Marz 1915" and simply "Schulz" on a smaller round marker near the parking lot.

Were these forgotten souls the ones responsible for the many haunting effects encountered by Valerie and others in the building?

Valerie was diagnosed as terminally ill from cancer and was in extreme discomfort most of the time, sometimes taking liquid morphine to subdue her pain. She was however not hallucinating and seemed perfectly aware and clear-minded about the whole affair. She has lived in that apartment for twelve years at the time of the investigation and claims that the phenomena start about eight or nine years after moving in.

She described seeing a man's shadow walking around in the kitchen while she was lying in bed. It was most definitely a male figure that she was sure of. Her rocking chair and baby toys have moved on their own dozens of times. As well as silverware, watches and personal items, some of these were becoming misplaced for awhile. Her front doorbell would often ring at 2 a.m. or in the middle of the afternoon and no one would ever be at the door. Friends and neighbors all knew of Valerie's condition and would always give her plenty of time to answer the door, so it obviously one of them. Plus a man's voice was also heard talking or holding a one-sided conversation in the living room and back bedroom.

A strange indescribable odor would often waft through the apartment and then quickly dissipate. Lights would turn on and off and her cat, Sebastian, would often arc its back, hiss and then scoot out of a room very quickly. Sometimes he would look upwards at the ceiling and follow something unseen with his eyes. One strange incidence was related by Valerie, "One time Bastian (short for Sebastian) screeched loudly and ran out of the back bedroom. Upon checking him, I found a patch of his hair missing at the back of his neck!" Indentations in both living room furniture and a bedroom chair were indications to Valerie that someone was seated on the upholstery.

One evening, a neighbor friend of hers, who was very skeptical of the stories that Valerie was telling her, had her own unique experience in the basement laundry room. Upon entering the darkened room which was well-illuminated by nearby streetlights and a full moon, she was shocked to see the figure of a man lying on the laundry room table enveloped in an eerie blue light. When the light switch was flipped, there was no one there! Needless to say, she changed her mind about doing the laundry that evening!

After my initial contact with Valerie, it seems things reached a peak. Sounds of things falling over in rooms became more pronounced and when investigating, she would find nothing amiss. The television and VCR would suddenly turn off in the middle of watching a rented movie as though the ghost wanted her full attention. "Punching" sounds on the walls and tall kitchen door were a new event and a male voice yelling as if in anger, yet indistinguishable was as heard. And, her niece and two nephews actually saw "him" standing in the kitchen. According to Valerie, he wasn't moving or doing anything, "just standing there, but for a long period of time. Longer than average!"

She began to call this apparition George, for lack of a better name. So when anything would happen, she would simply say that George was doing it and for him to stop scaring her. She even tried an Ouija board session, against my wishes, but she truly wanted to find out who the ghost was and what he/she wanted. She commented on her session as follows:

"I tried to give you as much info as I could on each 'spirit' we talked to. There were a few that came thru and tried to talk to us, but could only answer 'yes' or 'no' questions because they couldn't spell! Honest! I guess they didn't have proper schooling or none at all. We also communicated with some angry spirits and when they came thru, we tried to end it as soon as possible! I was told that whenever you use the Ouija board, before you release your hands from the board guide, you tell the spirit to look for the light and tell them they need to go into the light because that's where they belong. If you don't do this, the spirit may stay behind and wander."

According to her Ouija board session, she identified several possible ghosts haunting the property including Adam Thomas, who says he's the one she calls "George". He was born in 1523, died in 1583 and said that he and someone named Amanda was murdered by someone he didn't know. Adam told Valerie that he was worried about her, named her grandmother correctly and the lady who raised Valerie. He also said he <u>is</u> buried there. Zak Mekew who was born in France in 1602, came to America in 1627 and later died in 1655. He was married to Vairs (1610-1702), had three children and allegedly killed a man named Mat who fought over a woman. He was sentenced to death for the murder and hung. He also stated that he is buried on the property.

Eliga Reoc/Pebya (1917-1930) who was in the eighth grade when he was stabbed and killed. Sam Belb (1945-1960), from South Dakota, is also allegedly buried here. The angry ghost was called Tim Cweuh (1838-1877) and was married to Mary (1839-1912). Tim came here right after his birth. He said he was French but when asked what country he came from, it spelled out "Ngak". He also apparently killed a person, Lala. And the last spirit contacted, was a rapist, Dyb Peese (1933-1949), who came to America in 1936 and was killed by the brother of the girl he raped.

If the Ouija session is to be believed, then we has quite a few untimely and violent deaths perpetrated on the property in the past and would make an ideal spawning ground the ghost or ghosts.

Stanley Suho and Lucia Solis were brought in to help with the investigation as well as Pat Shenberg, clairvoyant. Extremely high EMF readings were indicated in several portions of the apartment correlating with the supernatural events that Valerie experienced. The show Sightings even did a segment here for the television show and brought along psychic, Peter Anthony who discovered psychic feelings both outside in the back yard (close to the gravestone markers) and downstairs in the basement. However, I was a bit skeptical of his psychic hits as he walked into Valerie's apartment at about the time she was describing her encounters for the Sightings cameras. He undoubtedly overheard some of her experiences which cast some doubts on what he later picked up.

The phenomena continued the entire time Valerie lived at the apartment until she moved out in March of 1999 to Ramsey, Illinois. Valerie claimed that as she was packing to move closer to her parents who could help take care of her, the phenomena became really bad as though George didn't want her to leave. She hasn't had any experiences at her new location so perhaps the ghosts just stayed in the same apartment, and, who knows, with the new tenants?

Kevin Cassidy House (former)
Chicago, IL.

A TV set and a gas stove turned on and off, furniture that repeatedly rearranged itself in a room and invisible hands that held two terrified young women down so they couldn't get up off a couch.

These eerie and unexplainable incidents have convinced Dr. Kevin Cassidy that his big, old house is haunted by the ghosts of two long-dead spinsters and other witnesses agree with him.

"I can tell you we've had a lot of spooky happenings here," said Dr. Cassidy, 50-year-old Chicago dentist. "I even had a priest come in to exorcize the place, but the place is still occupied by spirits. I still get the feeling I'm being watched, and get chills when I feel their presence."

Dr. Cassidy bought the 98-year-old, three-story, 11-room stucco house in 1980, and from the beginning felt it was scary.

"It looks like something out of a ghost movie, "he said. "Even the furniture looks strange, carved with grotesque gargoyles and other demonic-looking images. I did some research and found that two spinster maids named Great and Jane, who worked for the original owner, had died there.

"I first noticed something strange about the home during a Super Bowl party I threw for a bunch of friends. We were enjoying the game when one of my friends came back from the kitchen area. 'What's wrong with that room back there?' he asked. 'The house is warm, but that one room is so cold that even the water in the dog's bowl is frozen over and there are three radiators pushing out heat right next to it.'"

Dr. Cassidy said he turned up the heat but the room remained freezing cold for the next three weeks. He said he later learned that the room had once been occupied by the maid Greta.

Another night he was half asleep on his water bed when he suddenly felt someone sit down on the edge. "I felt the hair on the back of my neck rise and my whole body freeze," he said.

"I lunged to snap on the bedside light but there was no one there! I lay awake the rest of the night. The ghost never returned."

Another time he asked his secretary and office manager to finish up some paperwork at his home. The two women were sitting on a couch when the lights flickered off, then on again. The women became frightened, saying they felt they were being watched.

"They began to feel faint," Dr. Cassidy said. "They tried to get off the couch but couldn't. They were held back by strong invisible hands or forces."

At other times the TV set has switched itself on and off, gas burners have turned themselves on and off, and chairs have unexplainably shifted from one part of a room to another, the dentist revealed.

Pat LeBeau, a Chicago city fire fighter who's a friend of Dr. Cassidy, says he has 'felt the presence of spirits' while visiting the home.

"I've also seen lights go on and off, and seen furniture move, "said LeBeau, 59. "It's eerie!"

Unnerved by all the strange happenings, Dr. Cassidy called in a Catholic priest to exorcize the spirits and also a psychic to investigate the incidents. The psychic, Tony Vaci, who has helped Chicago police find missing persons and solve crimes, declared:

"There's no doubt about it. Dr. Cassidy's home is haunted. I could feel the house is full of spirits!"

Jack & Penny Young's Home
Reynolds, IL. 61279

Jack and Penny Young (not their real names) had lived in Reynolds, Illinois for approximately six years at the time of this investigation in March of 1996. The phenomena apparently started between thirty to forty years ago, as the Young's new the previous tenants and the owner. They were only renting this farm when they called the Ghost Research Society for help. No certain room of the house was the center of the activity however the upstairs closet, stairwell and kitchen were the most active. The farm is pre-Civil War, around the 1840s and perhaps even part of the Underground Railroad.

Apparitional figures included a shadow seen at the head of the stairs on the second floor and a strange mist was seen going towards the upstairs bathroom close to where the previous shadowy figure was observed. Penny saw a black shape of an old-time preacher in the kitchen dressed in period clothing and carrying a bible! The figure appeared to be quite solid and slowly vanished from sight. Sometimes referred to in rural areas as a "circuit preacher", he sported a black beard and long black hair.

Footsteps were heard in various parts of the home and lights turned themselves on and off. During the summer of 1993, a bed located in an upstairs bedroom shook violently by itself and frequent cold spots especially in the small closet upstairs were encountered. Doors and deadbolts locked by themselves, sometimes even locking out individuals at times. Tennis balls rolled across the floors without human or animal aid, even though they do own some dogs. A strange back-lit figure was also observed coming in from the backdoor around 2 a.m. which then proceeded to go upstairs towards the former servant's quarters. The figure had its hands at its side while it climbed the stairs. It was estimated at between 5'5" to 5'6" tall.

All the animals, including a cat, seem to react to something unseen at times and often don't wish to be left locked in the house alone. Eerie feelings, drafts, sounds and doors that swing open are other events reported by family members. Even a phantom voice which announced loudly, "I need to use the bathroom" was heard.

This farmhouse is located in a very remote section of western Illinois and is situated on many acres of land with a barn and horse stables nearby. The family genuinely seemed sincere and honest and were very helpful in pointing out areas of the house were past phenomena had occurred. The location was a virtual maze of stairways, rooms and an unfinished basement.

Stanley Suho, my wife and I visited the house with David Young (not his real name) who was our initial contact with this story. He provided us lodging information and directions to the house as well as treating us to a nice meal at a local restaurant.

After sweeping the entire house, it was apparent that there were exceptionally high electromagnetic fields in the kitchen, the stairs leading to the former servant's quarters and in the basement. The Negative Ion Detector, which picks up static electricity sometimes called negative ions, continued to register usually high static field readings around the sink area in the kitchen and the doorway to what was called the mudroom. The floor of both was of linoleum and shouldn't give off any evidence of static electricity because there was nothing there to generate that.

A camcorder was placed in the upstairs bathroom to monitor the hallway and area around the head of the stairs. Nothing unusual was recorded during the monitoring. A brief walk-thru was also filmed on videotape.

The Tri-Field Meter, which detects electromagnetic and electrical disturbances, was placed on a work bench in the basement and set to the electric setting which would then enable it to detect movements in electrical fields and act as a motion detector.

Suho placed a tape recorder next to the meter to monitor any disturbances. Later, a pronounced disturbance was indeed recorded as though someone or something had begun to approach the devices. No one went downstairs while the equipment was set up as the area was sealed off to everyone present.

The same devices were also later placed in an upstairs closet where cold spots and eerie feelings had been reported in the past. A similar, but no so pronounced, effect was also encountered and recorded. The closet was quite colder than the rest of the surrounding room. No psychic or ghost photographs were taken while there on the premises.

On a subsequent visit to the house, after the family had terminated their lease, with a cameraman from a television show, he felt extremely ill at ease when close to the house and did actually hear something fall over or drop while he was near the front door. Obviously, no one was in the house at the time.

This author does believe that the house probably has more than one ghost and it may indeed be a psychic imprint or residual haunting effect which continues to the present. Additional follow-ups with clairvoyants and/or an overnight stake-out would have been advantageous in discovering what exactly inhabits the house. Perhaps we shall never know for sure!

References

Downtown Haunts

Granny – *Chicago American July 29, 1936*
Haunted Castle – *"Noted Haunted Castle Once Stood at Corner of Archer and Western",*
Brighton Park Life, Golden Jubilee Supplement, May 18, 1939
Haunted Palace – *Chicago American July 2, 1936*
Elizabeth McCarthy House – *Chicago American July 22, 1936*
Old Robey Tavern – *Chicago Tribune August 8, 1900*
Rockwell Street Ghost – *Chicago American July 1936*

Northside Haunts

Dole Mansion – *Northwest Herald Article, October 10, 1997*
Duncan Avenue – *Copley Press, George Houde*
The Pale Horse – *Daily Gazette, March 16, 1874*
Tamerack – *Search International (www.search-international.com)*

Southside Haunts

Joliet Catholic High School – *"Priest's Spirit Haunts 'The Hill' Nearly 18 Years After*
Fiery Death." Joliet Herald News, John Whiteside, October 31, 1990
Maple Tree Inn – *"Maple Tree Inn in Blue Island Turns into Haunted Restaurant for*
Halloween." The Star, John K. Ryan, October 29, 2000
Mount Auburn Cemetery – *Visitors Guide to Beautiful & Historic Mt. Auburn*

Westside Haunts

Hotel Baker – *Chicago Sun-Times, Dan Rozer, October 31, 2000 – St. Charles Library*
Website
Masked Ghost – *"As For the Masked Ghost; Some See It, Some Don't." Suburban Trib,*
December 1, 1978

Legends and Short Stories

Willow Springs Fire Station – *History of Willow Springs*

Haunted Houses

Kevin Cassidy Home – *"Haunted House" National Enquirer, Paul F. Levy, April 18, 1989*

> Note: Although Ghost Research Society Press, Dale Kaczmarek, and all affiliated with this book have carefully researched all sources to insure the accuracy of the information contained in this book, we assume no responsibility for errors, inaccuracies or omissions.

Index

- ABOUT THE AUTHOR -
DALE KACZMAREK

DALE KACZMAREK is the President of the GHOST RESEARCH SOCIETY, an international organization of ghost researchers that is based in the Chicago area. He is the author of WINDY CITY GHOSTS and editor of a number of publications on ghosts and hauntings including, the now defunct Ghost Tracker's Newsletter, the Bibliography of Ghost Movies, National Register of Haunted Locations and others.

He has also contributed to and appeared in a number of occult-related books, including DEAD ZONES by Sharon Jarvis; THE ENCYCLOPEDIA OF GHOSTS AND SPIRITS by Rosemary Ellen Guiley; MORE HAUNTED HOUSES by Joan Bingham & Dolores Riccio; TRUE TALES OF THE UNKNOWN: THE UNINVITED by Sharon Jarvis; HAUNTED PLACES: THE NATIONAL DIRECTORY by Dennis William Hauck; SIGHTINGS by Susan Michaels and others.

Dale has made a number of television appearances on local and national news programs and has appeared in several documentaries on ghosts and haunted places, including "Encounters"; "Exploring the Unknown"; "The Other Side"; "Real Ghost hunters"; "Mysteries, Magic and Miracles" and many others. He has also appeared on dozens of radio programs and shows.

He is also the host of the EXCURSIONS INTO THE UNKNOWN Ghost Tours of Haunted Chicagoland locations. He currently resides with his wife Ruth in Oak Lawn, Illinois.

WRITE TO HIM IN CARE OF THE GHOST RESEARCH SOCIETY
PO Box 205, Oak Lawn, Illinois 60454-0205
Or Visit the GHOST RESEARCH SOCIETY Online at www.ghostreseach.org

ABOUT THE PUBLISHER
- GHOST RESEARCH SOCIETY PRESS -

GHOST RESEARCH SOCIETY PRESS was founded in 2005 and produces Print on Demand books for authors who have an interest in ghosts, hauntings and the paranormal and is located in Oak Lawn, Illinois. Files are produced professionally using state of the art programs and high-resolution scans. For further information contact us through the website.

GHOST RESEARCH SOCIETY PRESS
PO BOX 205
OAK LAWN, IL. 60454-0205
(708) 425-5163

GHOST RESEARCH SOCIETY ON-LINE

www.ghostresearch.org

CPSIA information can be obtained at www.ICGtesting.com
Printed in the USA
LVOW111503100413

328562LV00006B/514/A